Book Three
Perfect At Last Series

Perfect At Last
W E L L N E S S

Internal Calm
Amidst
External Chaos

Josephine Grace Chua Rojo, MD
Author

A Book Series, Book Three

Perfect At Last

WELLNESS

Internal Calm amidst External Chaos

Josephine Grace Chua Rojo, MD

Author

Table of Contents

Copyright Page

Perfect At Last book Series
Book Three
Perfect At Last WELLNESS, Internal Calm amidst External Chaos

First Printing: January 2020

Printed by:
Kanvess Digital Art & Graphic Design Studio
Unit 5B, 2ndLacson St., Bacolod City, Negros Occidental, Philippines, 6100

www.healthandwellnessforless.info
Join us on Facebook: Perfect At Last Support Group

Dedication

To you, whom I wish I have the time to talk to in person at any applicable time, through this book, I humbly share my sincerest thoughts that can possibly be of use to you. Know that all these come from a place of love and concern from someone who believes that we are all connected as one.

Acknowledgment

To my mother, *Julia*, and all the people I've known, both transient and permanent, thank you for being a part of my life.

Special thanks to my college professors, *Miss G (Flora Generalao), Miss Wency (Ma. Rowena Villarama-Mende), Sir Henry Francis Espiritu* and our late and most beloved, *Sir Mike Mende* for cultivating the side of me that I most treasure, and which led me to the making of this book.

To *Vishen Lakhiani* and *Mindvalley* for the affirmation and added inspiration.

Disclaimer

The information in this book is the sole opinion and belief of the author, written to the best of her knowledge and intentions. The bits and pieces of ideas that are laid out here were from the author's personal and vicarious experiences.

Some themes are universally known, but gathered here and organically created solely for the purpose of helping out a friend in need.

She/her, his/her or he/his alone refers to all sexes unless otherwise specified. No copyright infringement intended.

Preface

Growing up, I have a penchant for bottomless thoughts and self-reflection every time I learn from either personal experience, that of other people or from other possible theoretical sources. And this book is a summary of three decades worth of those moments that came from simple day to day stress to the struggles that may sometimes threaten the very existence of life.

Introduction

Positive psychology taught us that the secret to a happy life is to look at the glass as half-full, and not half-empty. But as someone who can objectively see it both ways, this dictum wasn't enough. Just like so many problems in this world, there is no one-size-fits-all answer. Each person is different and every scenario is as unique. It seems almost impossible that a universal solution can answer it all.

However, I personally believe in the power of the human mind, and how a mindset can make or break an individual. All of us have witnessed at least one person we thought would never do a certain thing, but did; or believed in certain people who eventually became the reason we became doubtful. On the contrary, we also saw firsthand how others picked up the pieces, succeeded and completely turned their lives from *nada* towards a triumphant end.

It doesn't matter whether you ran a multi-million company, a home-based business, or even if you are homeless. Your mental conditioning alone dictates whether you will live a stress-free life or a full one.

You see, I believe that everyone got what it takes to overcome whatever comes their way. But, not all have the lens to see the specific ways and means on how to exactly do it.

Your specific stressor may not be specified here, but I assure you that you can apply the key concepts in the following chapters that can make you take control of your being, your problems and eventually, your life, regardless of what you have on your plate right now.

Ten Core Values to Live the Most Fulfilling Life

1. Take responsibility for all the things that are happening to you. Never blame others, people, *God* or the situation, for any bad outcome.

2. Do your best in everything.

3. When you give, do it without any expectations.

4. Respect other's rights the way you want others to respect yours.

5. Know what you can and cannot control.

6. Have the courage to stand for what is intrinsically right.

7. Be brave to do what is necessary.

8. Let go of all the things that is beyond you and entrust it to a higher power.

9. Be mindful when preparing for possible undesirable outcomes and grateful when visualizing the best result.

10. Fill your thoughts with only positivity, joy, compassion, and love.

SECTION 1

Stress: Is It Mental or Physical?
Figuring Out this Ancient Enemy

"It's not the load that breaks you down, it's the way you carry it."

Lou Holtz

CHAPTER I

Instinctive Response to Modern-day Stress

"No man is free who is not master of himself."

Epictetus

During the recent 1% of human existence, the amount of mental, technological and scientific advancement cannot be equated to any other known progression ever recorded in history. This massive leap in evolution transformed the million-years-long apelike beings crushing stones into the scientists, builders, and astronauts we see today. Amazing as it may seem, it has its own drawback. A necessary review of evolution reminds us that genetic and physical adaptation to the changing environment takes hundreds of thousands of years before it can be apparent. Like the many animals seen by *Charles Darwin* in the

Galapagos Islands, the changes in the beak of certain birds in order to feed successfully where there are abundant food sources, or the lengthening of necks of giraffes depending on the height and luster of vegetation where they are frequently residing, all occurred after many generations of the same genetic line to experience the same sets of obstacles over and over again for it to finally have a genetic imprint and be physically expressed amongst the new generation.

To better see its process, just imagine the earlier *short-neck giraffes* that were already starving because all the leaves within their reach are already consumed. Thus, in order to survive, they have to aim high, tiptoed and stretched their necks as long as they can until they can reach their food at the top. That first giraffe that stretched its neck did not instantly develop a longer neck, neither does its offspring. But that offspring will do the same stretching of its neck and have another offspring, and another, and another, until after hundreds of years, multiple generations pass and finally, a long-necked giraffe is born that will start the new breed of giraffes we know today. This example is nothing but an understatement as compared to the complexity of human evolution.

To further appreciate this, let's take a look at a certain physical development in which we humans are more familiar with. Take, for example, the height of the nose bridge that largely differs between Asians and Caucasians, and this difference is accepted, but not really pondered upon by many as to why there is such. This difference, however, can be appreciated more when these races were labelled according to their geographic location, like those who live in the "tropics" and those in "cold" regions. This way, one can see the important factors such as weather and environment to the development of our body parts. In this context, the higher nose bridge will give more time for the air to be humidified and warmed before it enters the lungs because inhaling chilly air for long can injure the lung's lining if one doesn't develop a longer pathway. Meaning, a higher nose bridge has *survival value* in cold regions. This is not necessary for those living in the tropics because the air is already naturally humid. Thus, a shorter route, as manifested by a flat nose bridge, doesn't pose any risk, and is therefore just fit for survival. And yes, Asians born in cold countries will not magically grow higher nose bridges, simply because their genetic make-up did not adapt yet. But if they continue to live there consistently, their lineage in the next hundreds or perhaps thousands of years might end up just like the Caucasians are now.

However, I understand that the reason why you are reading this book is far more than the physical aspects of our humanity. As modern-day beings, we live and face daily modern-day problems like paperwork, deadlines, recital, a very difficult exam, traffic, business complexities, slow internet and many more. We feel anxious, we feel like we have no control. We do our best to do something about it. We get angry and frustrated when things aren't going our way, and in the end, we feel nothing else but stressed. You feel the blood rushing to your head, arms and legs as if you are about to engage in a fight or resort to flight. We sometimes even hear ourselves saying *"how I wish I can run away from it all"*, but, none of these you can do except sit still and wait, forcibly as patient as you can be. Worse, the stress keeps on building up inside, making you restless and uneasy most of the time.

This scenario may feel all too familiar, because one way or another, we've been on that road. We accepted it as a part of life and tried to deal with it using the modern ways we know (*like, asking the internet for answers*). But, what is really happening here? Why is it that no matter what the type of stress we face, we go through the same *rush-panic-stress-suppress-cycle*? Why does it feel like we are always running in circles? It is at this point that we have to take a closer look at ourselves. That no matter how contemporary you dress, or fancy you look, deep down, you, me, all of us, still are hardwired to have the instinctive response to stress the way our *hunter-gatherer ancestors* did for thousands, perhaps even millions of years of combined genetic experience.

Acknowledging this ideology will allow you to be more conscious of your actions, instinctive reactions and hopefully become better at managing them.

It is said that what separates us from other animals is our ability to act beyond what our instincts dictate. We are capable of higher cognition, processing and thought control. Unlike our other relatives in the animal kingdom, we are capable of not easily giving in to the five major instinctive "F" drives, namely: *fighting, fleeing, feeding, freezing and fornicating.*

Recognizing when any of these F's occurs is the key step for you to properly manage the task at hand, and thereby avoiding the unpleasant stress that these instincts bring. For example, when confronted with a problem, you feel uneasy and automatically activate the fight or flight response, but knowing this now, recognizing it and acknowledging that such response is no longer applicable to our modern-day challenges, you can consciously calm your nerves, think it through and clear your head until you can come up with a sound solution that is better than what your instinct tells you.

As *Epictetus* said, you can only be truly free once you've mastered your own self. Or maybe, you are already a master now (*only you can answer that honestly*).

But if you are uncertain, just like many of us, then right here, right now, this is a good start to begin this journey towards self-mastery.

CHAPTER II

Mental Stress with Physical Manifestation

"It is health that is real wealth and not pieces of gold and silver".

Mahatma Gandhi

With today's technology, news travels faster than any other means it used to. We may take advantage of the *feel-good stuff* you see on the internet, but one cannot deny the overwhelming bad news that also floods our timeline. News like suicide was previously only stigmatized amongst adults that are alone, lonely, with grave problems (*like unemployment, marital or other personal concerns*). But nowadays, it is no longer a surprise to hear young adults, and even teens to resort to that grave end. Although the increased incidence may just be due to reporting bias, *because we wouldn't really know for sure how many young ones succumb to such option prior to the advent of social media*, one cannot deny the importance of mental health that directly links to this physical damage.

It is said that ***the best gift of life, is life itself***. And it is very disheartening to hear of another soul, especially the young ones, giving up the very gift that life has given them.

But, physical damage does not only occur in death or in illness. Sometimes, the damage is not that apparent. Stress attacks a person in all forms, and oftentimes, in the most inconspicuous way that we ourselves hardly notice. These may include the difficulty of sleeping or too much of it, under or overeating, obsessive-compulsive behaviors like *hoarding* or inability to let go of things. Sometimes, it manifests as suddenly feeling negative about something you previously anticipated.

If we do not deal with these emotions head-on, this little nuisance is enough to ruin your day.

And one bad day can easily lead to another. Stress hormones can surge persistently and these can start a vicious cycle that can now have apparent physical manifestations like skin breakouts, undesired weight loss/gain, looking older, falling hair, bowel disturbance, irritability, and lack of focus, poor performance, even tumor growth and much more.

Indeed, there is no greater relief than reversing all these without the need for medications, surgery or any other external factors other than the **cure** that is already **within you**. But before we go into the details, let us also recognize our enemy here: *stress* and *negativity*.

One of the best war advices has been to never underestimate your enemy because it is the only way that you can come prepared, or better yet, over-prepared.

In a behavioral experiment published in 2005 entitled *"Chewing on it can chew you up: Effects of Rumination on Triggered Displaced Aggression"* by Bushman et al, it was shown that those group of people who were provoked by a minor annoyance and were given time to ruminate (*or to think deeply and negatively*) later on responded more aggressively when another minor annoyance was presented, as compared to the other group who was distracted and was not given time to ruminate about the first annoyance. This only shows how negativity can lead to an even graver kind of negativity that can eventually jeopardize your own sanity. This is a very basic reason why it is always recommended to just brush off negativity whenever you can.

As a believer in evolutionary psychology, I am inclined to consider that this human response actually has survival value. That is, when one somebody upsets you, you become more alert the next time they will do the same thing so that he/she will be apprehended from doing the same unpleasant thing to you again. And yes, I know that you probably feel that you've succeeded in that sense, but when you try to examine this scenario closely, you will see that you also lost in some way. This is because *surrendering to negativity* can only solidify the need for future negativity. And unknowingly, you may sadly become the person you are feeling unpleasant towards. Others may not notice it, but eventually, one might just be surprised when the room starts to clear, or silences whenever they arrive. It is an undesirable thing to be that person others avoid, and this is just one part of the vicious cycle, we will try to get as far as we can as we proceed in the chapters ahead. Do not worry as there is still hope for those who you know to be trapped in this disheartening cycle of pessimism. It will not be easy, but know that it is possible and very much doable, should you simply keep an open mind.

I hope right now you start to brush off some heavy feelings you have because it will only get better from here. This point will be your starting point in going towards a positive future and onwards a better life.

CHAPTER III

Physical Stress with Psychological Impact

"Health is a state of the body. Wellness is a state of being."

J. Stanford

Sometimes, no matter how good your state of mind is, even that personal sense of balance can still be disrupted by physical stress.

When one is physically working beyond what the body can take, there will come a point that one will break down if a *needed rest* is not initiated before it is too late.

Not all kinds of stress can be answered with just mental adjustment. But the right mindset can make a person manage stress successfully and continue to be functional while dealing with it. A right mindset can allow one to avoid going to that deep hole of fatigue and restlessness.

Over fatigue can happen both from too much work and a lack of enough rest. Sometimes, when your body needs rest, but you do not respond accordingly (*most common reason is the supposed "lack of time"*), it will drive your mind to overcompensate on other things. For many, the most common *go-to* substitute is food. Others are in the form of material things like shopping or drinking, and sadly, for some, they can resort to illicit drugs. The problem with these kinds of alternatives is that they do not address the core deficiency, which is resting. Yet, they activate the fragile pleasure center in our brain and overshadowing its true need. As a result, one tends to keep on doing it; some even to a point of addiction that we all know can cause damage not just to the person but also to everything else he/she is connected to.

In the succeeding sections, we shall discuss how to manage time and what are the ways and means of acquiring more of it, and how to generate productivity without resorting to destructive behaviors.

Meanwhile, listen to your body. Be mindful when your body is telling you to rest, to stop, or be still. It is one of the most important aspects a person must be a master of within himself.

CHAPTER IV

Material Problems Affecting One's Well-being

"Although difficult, change is always possible. What holds us back from making the changes we desire, are our own limiting thoughts and actions."

Satsuki

So far, we have covered the instinctive, mental and physical sources of stress. But in this modern world, we have types of stress that are not as apparent in the old world. It may have its own counterpart in the past, *like territories to hunt, caves to occupy, the sharp spears to have or the best animal coat to use.* But today, the stress from material things largely occupies the reason why people's wellbeing is compromised.

Although there are many other material things in this world, here, for the sake of discussion, we will use a universal currency and that is *money*. It is deemed so important that money becomes the reason for living for some and as a result, also becomes the major stressor.

I do not believe that wanting to have wealth and prosperity is bad. To properly evaluate one's attachment to monetary values, one should focus on the "***why***" or the "***what for***" of getting rich *like the ability of helping others or uplifting the lives of the family*, rather than having it as the end goal. Because, if one focuses on the wrong motivation in attaining money and give in to greed, then he is surely doomed to fail.

Studies show that a lot of suicides were linked to stress brought about by debts and financial catastrophes. Some who were able to counter such life-threatening thoughts had no choice but engage in an unhealthy option in order to temporarily address a problem, despite long-term side effects.

Yes, money is a universal need because it is a basic commodity so that one can live decently.

But, you should believe that although money is sometimes a problem, it should not become an impossible problem.

However, if at this moment you already have deep money problems, know that it has a solution. It will be specifically discussed in the later chapters, but I humbly suggest you read through the next sections first as they are deemed necessary in order for you to properly execute what you needed to do. That is, by ripening into the right mindset at the right time.

Accept that wealth and riches are neutral. It only becomes good or bad depending on how you use it. So, if your heart is in the right place, do not stop yourself from wanting riches. Welcome it with open arms and believe that you deserve it. It is only with this secured mentality that abundance can come through.

Yes, there is hope. Always remember that if you already feel you are at your lowest, then there is nowhere else to go now but up. Just hang in there because you are about to change your life with some techniques that can clear away what we call as "*abundance blocks*".

Keep an open mind and you will be blessed with the right kind of abundance, in all forms.

SECTION 2

Two Things You Need to Know to Overcome a Thousand Stressor

"The day she let go of the things that were weighing her down, was the day she began to shine the brightest."

Katrina Mayer

CHAPTER V

Choosing an Internal Locus of Control Makes You in Control

"Man needs difficulties. They are necessary for health."

Carl Jung

It is said that what makes a situation *stressful* is the *uncertainty* of it.

Like in any disorders, nature versus nurture is also considered in Pathological Psychology. Wherein, those with a genetic or familial predisposition in developing a disorder, *like anxiety*, have greater chances of having one as compared to those who don't. Again, this doesn't mean a definite route because environmental factors may also contribute to whether or not such disorder will be expressed. As you can see, some siblings have it, and some don't, which only goes to show that certain unique experiences shape an individual differently.

It is where the perceived *locus of control* comes in. When a person experiences something unpleasant, there is automatic and unconscious processing that goes on in one's head. The negative scenario is assessed and the following questions are asked:

- *Is it because of me?*

- *Did I cause my own suffering?*

- *Is it somebody else's fault?*

- *Am I suffering because of circumstance, fate or other things I am not in control of?*

- *Who will I blame?*

If you can, try to think of a situation that made you feel unpleasant recently, you can take this time to answer the following questions too. It would be best for you to put it in writing to better appreciate the scenario.

If everybody is honest enough with themselves, a lot actually puts the blame on external factors, like other people, the circumstance and even God. Such blame that is put *away* from the "*self*" is actually understandable, because the *opposite*, which is putting the blame *towards* one's self, would affect the person's own confidence, and even identity. Wrongly doing so may lead to self-doubt, poorer performance, and even more stress.

However, there is a large drawback to this kind of thinking. This is because it makes the person's self-confidence intact, but does NOT promote growth and development.

If one shifts the locus of control ***internally***, that is, putting the "blame" towards one's self for a certain unpleasant outcome, the person can then thoroughly examine each process in that negative experience, break it down into details and identify which aspects he committed some lapses and which items he can improve.

To do this, one can try to answer the following questions to aid internal locus of control and at the same time constructively improve himself for future use.

- *At which point did I take part in that unpleasant event?*

- *Knowing the displeasing outcome now, what could have I done to change it?*

- *If there are other alternative scenarios, what can I do to be more prepared?*

- *For the things that are out of my control, what could have I done to improve it?*

- *What can I do to keep this from happening again in the future?*

Going back to your own personal experience, you can *reexamine* the situation by looking at it using a different lens through these questions. Compare your answers side by side and see how it differs.

Can you see how both mindsets have different feels in the end? Because when one claims control over the scenario, even if it has not physically manifested yet, but with a kind of control that is internally focused, there is a subsequent **increase** in his sense of **security and stability**.

As one shift to internal, rather than external locus of control, the perceived degree of certainty increases, the positivity towards a better outcome increases, and eventually, the level of stress decreases.

That is generally a great thing. But, there is a catch to this if one does it wrongly. That is, *blaming oneself without counteractive resolve to improve it*, or worse, stays on the "blaming" period that has the tendency towards depression. It is at this point that it should be emphasized that if things went sideways, and you took part in it, accept it, whether it was intentional or not, forgive yourself and make a resolution to make good next time. Weep if you must, but make sure you move on afterward. It is vital you realize that each step you take towards the right decision is a step closer to a better and brighter day.

Now, how about when there are *repeated* un-*pleasantries* despite having an internal locus of control? Then, simply do the same steps again because, remember, each situation is unique and no two scenarios are exactly the same. Thus, there will always be a room for improvement. Once you are able to identify what went wrong and how you could have prevented it or reacted to improve it, then you can be assured that when this similar thing happens again, you will be able to see it coming. And this time, things are going to be different, in a good way.

Bonus: Other than visualizing the scenarios as if playing and replaying a video in your head, you can also try to practice meditation. A simple 10 minutes of silence each morning while only focusing on your breathing can already improve your sense of well-being. This simple practice can improve one's intuition and foresight, which are key concepts in developing wisdom that can eventually help one lead the best possible life that is aligned with his/her innate gifts and purpose.

CHAPTER VI

Letting go of the Wrong Things will Set Things Right

"When a man is ill, his very goodness is sickly."

Friedrich Nietzsche

The concept of letting go of anything that causes the negativity (*the bad, the dark, the ugly or simply the wrong stuff*) has always been one of the most common pieces of advice given to everyone. And this may sound overrated, but it actually is one of the core concepts that we must internalize if we wish to live a life that is happy and free.

However, it may not come as easy or as successful for some, simply because it will take a certain degree of courage to even start this. You will know that it is not easy because there are many people who are guilty of hanging on to negativity and even have the habit of multiplying it. *If you don't believe me, start by trying to imagine that one friend who cannot stop complaining about anything and everything that is happening around.* The one who keeps on pointing what is wrong with this or that. There is that person who is very vocal with things that need improvement rather than appreciating the good side, the one who seems to love bursting other people's bubbles. Or, you can also check with yourself. Be honest and ask yourself if this person could be you? Are you always seeing the negative in everything? Are you always the one called as the best "critique" or just the one who has that "eye" best fitted in the "fault finding" committee? (*Remember the effect of* **rumination**, *as mentioned before.*)

Don't get me wrong, it is not bad to see the negative. In fact, it is a gift that can be maximized in helping and uplifting others and things around you. However, not everybody uses it that way. When you are able to see the negative, say for example a bad fashion combination, if you say it hastily, the person will feel bad about it, thinking that your only motive behind is to make him feel bad and equally showing off that you have good taste. Instead, do it to help, by telling the person in private that what he is wearing maybe the most comfortable clothes, but how it looks could have been improved by doing this or that, so it will be more pleasant, more appropriate and representative of the decent being as you know him to be. This way, you are letting go of negativity within you and at the same time generating positivity by converting it to something good.

Now, moving on to the details, how can one let go of certain things at the right time?

The *first thing* that you need to do is go about your day as normally as you would. Then, keep track of anything that made you feel negative, no matter how small. For every incident that *made you feel unpleasant*, whether it is a rock you accidentally stepped on, an unfriendly receptionist, or a negative comment from someone you know, ask yourself this: *Can I do something about this?* If the answer is "**Yes**", then **do** what you have to do. If the answer is "**No**", then just simply **let it go** and whisper to the universe that everything is alright in the end. If the answer is maybe, because you are uncertain whether something can really be done or you are not willing to do what it takes, then ponder on it. Give yourself a short time to decide and categorize it to either a yes or a no.

Remember, that when you decide that you can do something about it, make sure that your approach to it is a way that will convert a negative experience into something positive. Thus, without raising a voice, or exerting too much physical effort, just smile, and do it. This way, you are taking control of the situation by taking responsibility for the part that you claim. Do this without overstepping into another person's shoe and you'll see your day getting better.

But, how about if things did not turn out as planned? Or it gets worse? Then, you simply go back to the same process just like the first. When you still consider it as a "Yes, I can do something about it", then do. Maybe you did the best thing you thought is best at that time, but in hindsight, you could have done something better, and this time is the chance to really do it better.

On the other hand, once you decide that it is beyond your control, whether you can't do something about it literally *(like a massive rock you cannot lift)*, or simply an unpleasant person you do not want to deal with, then, with a deep breath, exhale a little longer and let that go. Again. Let. It. Go.

Once you have decided to let it go, inhale deeply, and welcome the air of positivity coming in, and feel the happiness as if the unpleasant scenario never occurred at all. Then, give thanks, *(either to God, to the higher being that you look up to or to the universe)* for this specific time that you felt lighter from letting it go. Doing so will not only give you the instant positivity that you need, but you also welcome more positivity that comes your way. Sooner or later, things will just fall into place. It's not like *'you will no longer feel unpleasant ever again'*, but it is having the capacity to correct that feeling and converting an unpleasant incident into an experience that goes deep into self-discovery and positivity. This is a basic foundation of how one can achieve an internal calm amidst external chaos. Become a source of positivity instead of the opposite. *Radiate goodness and welcome betterment as it naturally comes back*.

And as you finish your day, always allow time to reflect, to be one with your thoughts and examine each aspect of your life. Just like the way you did to the unpleasant things you encountered, make a step back and view your life from afar as well.

Try to feel and see things in your life and recognize which things make you feel good, hopeful, dreamy, thankful, and happy. On another end, see what things, aspects of your life or which people make you feel unpleasant and negative that seems to be limiting you from attaining that state of *peace* or "*nirvana*". Identify, and then, apply this question: *Do I know the answer to this problem? Can I do something about it?* Then, categorize your answer to just either a "YES",

"POSSIBLE" (or maybe) and "IMPOSSIBLE" (or no). Next, convert the possible and commit to either a "yes" or a "no". Do what you have to do for the "yes", and let go by entrusting the universe all the things that you cannot do anything about, and embrace the best possible outcome as if it already happened. :)

To wrap things up as we end this section, we go back to the two things a person needs to do to overcome any stressor that may come your way. As you face a stressor, categorize whether it is a "Yes, I can do something about it" and "No, it's beyond my control"

1. For the Yes, simply take responsibility, have an **internal locus of control** (*while making sure you are not doing it in a publicly bragging and annoying way*). Be secure in your own thoughts that whatever may happen, you did the best you can. For whatever unpleasant things in the past where you took responsibility, forgive yourself. Make a commitment to do better the next time around.

2. For the NO, then, just ***let go, have faith*** and ***trust*** the universe that everything will be alright, and feel the positivity as if everything is already in its perfect place and time.

As what *Steve Jobs* said: *"You can only connect the dots looking backwards"*. Who knows, such negative episodes may actually tie you to something great in the future. Simply close each phase of letting go with a little whisper and hope that whatever you desire, or something even better, will unfold.

SECTION 3

Three Things You Need to Do to Execute *"Project: Happy You"*

"Happiness is when what you think, what you say and what you do are in harmony."

Mahatma Gandhi

CHAPTER VII

First, Make Self-Care a Priority

"Loving yourself isn't vanity. It's Sanity"

Katrina Mayer

Some say that self-care and self-love is just a reflection of vanity. However, I disagree. Rather than vanity, self-love is no shorter than a necessity. It is something that any living soul should embark on. It is embedded in our genes to survive and part of that survival is living a happy, fulfilling and purposeful life. And one cannot simply do so without ensuring his own wellness first.

True, it can be vanity, but only if one focuses on the wrong things as motivation to self-love. That is, looking good for others to see, in hope of envy or just simply to show off. But, when the reason behind goes beyond the person, which is, attaining your best self, to eventually become of service for a higher purpose without considering what you can get in return, then *self-love becomes a selfless act.*

By taking good care of yourself, you can do your job better, you can be of aid to those who are in need, you can maximize your potential, and your capacity to engage in a productive cause, will not be put at risk.

Parents can raise their young and ensure that they see them in adulthood. Teachers can educate more and mold better leaders for our future. Workers and businessmen can continue to provide for their families. Artists can move millions by inspiring them to get in touch with their humanity. Preachers can spread goodness to many, especially those who are in dire need of support. Doctors can only save more the moment they are well taken care of as well. And you can multiply the good things you already do only after you make self-care a priority too.

Whether passion, advocacy or profession, you can become a beacon that can inspire those around you by first taking care of *you*.

Seriously engage in self-love now, and see that everything else will fall into place afterwards.

Prioritizing Health

Are you currently studying, working, practicing your craft, or managing a business? Is it going well? Or is the future still uncertain? Do you have a loving family you adore so much? Or are you in a vocation of positively impacting the lives of many?

Many of us are all caught up and engrossed with our day to day activities that we often overlook our current medical and psychological health. We have been busy living and trying to make our way to materialize the dreams we have for ourselves and our loved ones that we sometimes take the "little stuff" like adequate sleep and proper diet for granted. Those goals mostly include acquiring certain rewards and personal achievements that our hearts desire the most. However, sometimes, during the process of focusing on the end goal, we miss an essential aspect that can jeopardize all that we ever worked hard for, and that is our *health*.

Imagine 20 or 40 years from now, you already have the dream house you always wanted, with cars and a bank account that can allow you to travel the world. You have a beautiful family that loves you and you love more, with a status that enables you to do what you are passionate to do. However, by this time, can you also imagine yourself physically active and strong? With the stamina that allows you to take the stairs to enjoy the view from your rooftop every sunset? Or being able to sustain hours playing with your grandchildren? Or the long hike in the streets of Europe or The Great Wall without losing your breath? Or able to do yoga at your 60s? If yes, then you are on the right track. However, if you're not so sure, then it's about time you take a pause, assess your priorities and think about the bigger picture.

You see, whatever you decide to focus and dedicate your life to, it will only be up to a certain point unless you do whatever you can do to make sure you will be there, alive and with the strength to savor it! Whether it is missionary work to help those who are in need, humanitarian effort to liberate those who are oppressed, service to family and friends, raising children to become responsible adults or a personal journey to self-fulfillment, it is a core value to take good care of your own health, because without it, none of it will materialize for long.

There is no-one else in this world that will make your own health care a priority without an ulterior motive, other than yourself. Because without good health, it is such a heartbreak to only imagine the expansion of your enterprise, the places you could have explored, the people whom you could have helped and spend time with or how your children will turn out to be, if you will no longer be there to actually witness it.

We only have one life. We only have this one chance to really live it. Whether we decide to dedicate it to others or to ourselves, we ought to make sure we stay in the prime of our health in order for us to eventually witness and savor the fruits of our labor on our senior years firsthand. Let us celebrate life by first taking good care of it.

Importance of Sleep

"Sleep is the golden chain that ties health and our bodies together."

Thomas Dekker

One part of the basic essentials of living is to rest, and there is no better way to do it than sleeping. It is the only way that your body, hormones, and especially your brain cells can regenerate so it can function optimally for the next day. It is considered as a biochemical necessity and a very important component of living, across the animal kingdom.

Studies show that a perpetual lack of sleep can lead to a shorter lifespan. Whether you are a night owl or an early bird, as long as you are able to get 7-9 hours of continuous sleep each day, you'll be able to maximize your day given that you've had a restful sleep.

The following are some of the insights on sleeping that can help us prioritize it more:

1. Know your body well and note when you are most productive: Daytime or Nighttime. Each of us has a natural tendency, when we are most active. Good thing we can also learn to still be productive at a different time if necessary. (*I myself am a night owl, but has adapted to function during daytime since my job requires me to*). Just be secured with the idea that it is not a sign of laziness if you are not an early riser, as long as you are not causing a hassle to anyone and you are functioning optimally once you are up and awake.

2. Appropriate your work with your sleep schedule when you can. However, if it is not feasible, then, adjust your sleeping patterns accordingly. For example, if you are an early bird, a morning person that has all the energy during the day, but takes on an important job on a graveyard shift, you can adjust your sleeping schedule during the day so you will have adequate rest still. Likewise, for night owls, those who function at their best at night and have a day job, you too can adjust. Some of us mostly choose to stay up and just force ourselves to wake up early thinking that we can fully function still. And most of the time, out of habit, we really can. But we should do it less, as studies show that chronic lack of sleep or habitually sleeping for only less than 6-7 hours a day is linked to an early death. Thus, even if we think we are maximizing our time in a day, we might actually be risking our life as a whole by shortening it in years.

3. Eight hours of sleep is not an exact science. One can feel worse when awakened in the middle of a sleep cycle. On average, a full sleep cycle is about an hour and 30 minutes (*90-110 minutes*). After each deep sleep, there is a short period of light sleeping in between that ~90-minute cycle, where you can be easily awoken. So, if you have an alarm, set it to a time that is a multiple of 90 minutes and you will see how you will wake up easily and not irritably. Thus, 7 hours and 30 minutes to about 9 hours of sleep are the goals. Set your alarm at 6, 7.5or 9 hours of sleep every day, depending on your schedule so that you will wake up just in time that a full 90-minute sleep cycle has ended. (*You may adjust this accordingly once you're able to see a pattern when you will feel most rested.*)

4. The benefits of having adequate sleep cannot be overemphasized. To enumerate,

these will include the following, plus many more:

- Reduces stress and improves mood

- Helps in weight management

- Increases focus, memory and overall mental functioning

- Slows down aging and makes the skin more radiant

- Rejuvenates up to the cellular level by decreasing the risk for cancer development

- Aids in healing

- Improves overall well-being

5. Otherwise, the lack of sleep is linked to the following ill-effects

- Irritability

- The risk of developing depression and other psychiatric disturbance

- Poor mental focus and memory

- Poor physical performance

- Weight gain

- Associated with cancer, and other lifestyle diseases (hypertension, diabetes, obesity)

- Impairs judgment

- Decreased self-control, that is, prone to be persuaded by others and vulnerability to the power of suggestions

- Early death, by accidents or illness

Thus, sleep should become a priority, as basic as water, good food and clean air.

Therapeutic, NOT Emotional Eating

"Eat to live, not live to eat."

Socrates

Contrary to sleep, food is something that we prioritize a little more than we need. That is, we take in more food than our body actually needs.

If one becomes sensitive enough to listen to their bodies, you will know that cutting our food intake in half is actually more beneficial for our overall well-being when considering the aspect of true health and healing. (*The details of having a better relationship with food are written in detail in Perfect At Last WEIGHT and Perfect At Last HEALTH books, the first two parts of this series, to which I personally suggest that any adult should read.*)

For the purposes of wellness and how it is also influenced by our mealtime practices, we will discuss the importance of eating and how food can be used for sustainable healing when eaten in moderation and how other foods can become a quick fix that is even more potent than some illicit drugs.

You see, there are three major macronutrient categories of foods, namely, fats, proteins, and carbohydrates. Fats include all oily substance and common examples include butter, bacon, egg yolk, animal fats, and cooking oils. Proteins include lean meat, most seafood, egg white, mushrooms, beans, and nuts. Natural carbohydrates include most fruits and vegetables while the processed or cultured ones include bread, pastries, sugar, rice, pasta, and sweetened drinks. You may wonder why we need to know this when we are talking about wellness. This is because not all foods affect you the same way.

Every time you eat food, it could trigger three different sensations in your body: 1) sense of satisfaction when you've had enough, 2) sense of fullness from your stomach lining when it is stretched from being full and lastly, 3) sense of pleasure from your taste buds. Proteins and fats are the two food groups that activate the sense of satisfaction on your "Satiety Center" even before you can feel the stretch from your stomach lining. Thus, if you are sensitive enough, you will avoid overeating and stop eating even before your stomach feels heavy enough that you unable to take in a deep breath. (*But depending on the preparation and the amount of salt, it can give a lot of sense of pleasure too*).

However, carbohydrates, especially in the form of sweets, only trigger the "*Pleasure Center*" in our brain without activating the *Satiety Center*. This is the same pleasure center that is highly active among other addictions like illicit drugs, alcohol, gambling, sex, and even shopping! As a result, we tend to consume sweets and more carbs than we ever need and we stop only when our stomach lining is fully stretched that we can no longer take another bite. And most often, we find ourselves saying "*I'd still love to eat some more, it's just that my stomach cannot take it anymore*". This also explains why after eating a full meal, one can no longer eat another slab of steak, but can still accommodate a slice of cake. In the end, we see a lot of lifestyle diseases and problems that are associated with high sugar intake, including mood instability and chemical imbalance in our brain.

Can you see now how this food can be a source of temporary comfort, but can lead to destructive results? Unfortunately, whenever we feel down, we always go to food as a source of comfort rather than confronting the root cause of such unpleasant event, and superficially *"satisfy"* our pleasure center as a means to compensate. But knowing the science behind it, we can now be more conscious whenever we eat and maybe think twice before we give in to such food vulnerability. Take control and be free from food slavery.

I am not saying to never eat whenever you feel bad. However, you can first confront the problem first-hand the way we discussed in the previous section and deal with it in our head before directly proceeding to food as an immediate transient respite. Once dealt, you can indulge in food, but this time, you can avoid overeating unhealthy food choices but still satisfy your need to feed.

Here are some tips you can do to have a more fulfilling food experience and lesser chances of having regretful episodes of comfort eating:

1. Know when you're really in need of food nutritionally, and not just *eat* simply because it is "*time to eat*". According to *Eric Edmeades* of WildFit, we have to acknowledge the other types of *hunger* that might fool us into thinking that it is **real nutritional hunger**. These are **dehydration hunger** (from water and salt), **hypoglycemia** (from transient decrease from low blood sugar after getting used to elevated blood sugar for a long time), **empty stomach syndrome** (not because it is empty, doesn't mean you are already in need of food because it might take about 12 hours or longer for your food to stay in your lower intestinal system before the nutrients are fully absorbed), and lastly, **emotional hunger** (or even *boredom*, where the

root cause should be addressed and not answered by food).

2. Eat first the foods that are nutrient-dense, high in natural fats and proteins to give you the satisfaction you need.

3. Make sure to add adequate salt to make the taste satisfactory. Studies show that most sugar cravings are actually produced by low salt in the body and consuming some salt can cure sugar cravings.

4. Eat or drink low-calorie foods that can fill in your stomach. The simplest forms would be water and green leafy vegetables.

5. After all this eating, try to skip dessert. But you can have some only if you find it really necessary. And this time, most likely, you will be able to consume only less than you normally would.

Incorporating Fasting and Exercise

"Periodic fasting can help clear up the mind and strengthen the body and the spirit."

Ezra Taft Benson

Exercise has been one of the well-documented modes of improving mental health and an overall sense of well-being. By definition, exercise is the repeated movements of large muscle groups that generate energy. Just doing moderate physical activity like jogging or brisk walking for 30 minutes, five times a week is already said to be enough to maintain optimum health. Other than the physical benefits, exercise has been shown to improve the chemical imbalance in the brain seen in those suffering from depression, anxiety, and other psychological disorders. And with determination, one can incorporate exercise in their daily lives. Yes, I know it may sound so tiring at first. A good thing that by just starting from two minutes a day, as an effective means to start something or the concept known as *"mini habits"* popularized by *Stephen Guise*, you can truly exercise daily and consistently. This mini-habit is enough to potentially develop into a more established habit. And with the advent of *HIIT or High Intensity Interval Training*, it is said that a 4-minute HIIT can already provide you with the benefits that is equivalent to that of 30-minute brisk walk. This is by doing a 20-second HIIT (*like a rigorous jumping jack or plank*) and a 10-second rest. Do this for 8 continuous cycles and it will give you a total of only 4 minutes with enough cardio workout. This set is what we've been practicing for a while now and so far it feels great, especially that 4 minutes is easy to be inserted on a schedule.

Yet, for various reasons, not everyone has the luxury to do it as religiously as others still, despite the concept of "mini habits", either for lack of time, motivation or even physical disability. Good thing, current studies on neurology shows that there is another way to improve cognitive function and mood the way exercise does even without lifting a finger. And surprisingly, it is through *fasting*.

Millions of years ago, our ancestors survived recurrent episodes of prolonged hunger and starvation as hunters and gatherers. Over time, our genes as humans adapted, enabling us to survive long periods of no food intake. This way, our body adjusted making fasting generally safe when done right, and such is now contentedly backed up by science.

However, with the agricultural and industrial revolution during the last 1% of human existence, we were exposed to the sudden and widespread availability of food that the normal *periods of no food intake* already sounded like an obsolete practice. Except for religious reasons, *fasting*, or the intentional decision of not eating any caloric-containing or sweet-tasting food and drinks for more than 12 hours becomes a taboo. The best thing though, that the current generation is already starting to explore and see the benefits of fasting. Now that its popularity is increasing, many are now deliberately incorporating *fasting* into their day to day life.

With various trends, fasting has evolved to have many terminologies depending on lengths or the type of stuff you allow to take during that period. The most common type would be *intermittent fasting*, wherein one divides the 24 hours in a day into an eating window and a fasting period. For example, the 16:8 schedulescan be done by *fasting* for 16 hours daily and only eats or drinks during the next 8 hours. This may sound extreme for some, but for regular *fasters* like me, this is just normal. In fact, it is already as effortless as breathing and eating more than that period already upsets my stomach. And it can be anyone's normal too should you be open to it. To see it from another perspective, one can have his last bite for dinner at 6PM and can have breakfast after 10AM the next day and have an 8-hour eating window from 10AM-6PM. It can be adjusted accordingly and have different variations as well.

Personally, I started at 16:8 and eventually embarked on multiple extended fasting (*as long as 10.5 days on water only, literally not eating anything except water*). And currently, my regular day consists of a minimum of 19 hours fasting and an eating window of only 5 hours at maximum. Shortening my fast below that is already an exemption rather than the rule. It is a wonder how I feel at my most functional self when I consume the *minimum sustenance*, at least a lot less as compared to what the food industry is trying to sell us.

Although not as popular now because of business and politics, fasting has been studied in the medical field and its various benefits have been established. This very practice can even resolve many of the lifestyle diseases we see today.

The following are the known benefits of fasting, but there are many more not mentioned here;

- Fasting is **affordable**, you do not need to spend anything to do it.

- Fasting gives you more **time** because it will eliminate the time needed to think about what to eat, to prepare, to finally eat, to clean our dishes, and the time we take to relax after eating.

- Fasting can double your **productivity**.

- Once adapted, fasting leads to **improved** memory and mental performance.

- Fasting heals the body.

- Fasting can be done **safely** by almost everyone (*except very young, growing children, pregnant women, and in select cases*).

- Fasting is a natural **weight loss** technique.

- Fasting improves overall **well-being** by taking control of one's being.

- Fasting is as good as **exercise** neurologically.

- Fasting is a great way to practice **temperance**.

- Fasting **heals** diabetes.

- Fasting can **wean** some peopleof their medications for hypertension and elevated cholesterol.

- Fasting improves **mood** when done right.

- Fasting heals Polycystic Ovarian Syndrome or **PCOS**.

- Fasting heals allergies and other signs of **inflammation**.

- Fasting can be a form of **meditation**.

- Fasting can lead some to a sense of **enlightenment**.

- Fasting provides an avenue to exercise discipline and **patience**.

- Fasting reduces one's carbon footprint and eventually **saves** animals, nature and earth.

These and many more are the benefits of fasting. Once incorporated into one's life, the potential to improve your overall being is limitless.Learning about and embracing *fasting*as a way of life has been one of the most important life-changing events that happened to me in my adult life. It paved the way to everything else that I have now, including this book. *My fasting anniversary is something that I celebrate now more than my own birthday because the day I practiced it felt like the start of a brand new and better life.*

A word of warning, *fasting* should not be done hastily. It should be a guided one as this can be dangerous when done without the right mental and physical preparation. Good thing, everything is now available online. But if you wish to have it in a one-look source, the necessary details of fasting are carefully detailed and can be pleasantly read in the book one of this series (*Perfect At Last WEIGHT*).

By doing the ones enumerated above, plus your own insights on self-care, you become inevitably set to conquer all forms of successes that life has in store for you.

CHAPTER VIII

Second, Tap Your (Multi-) Potentials

"The only person you are destined to become, is the person you decide to be."

Ralph Waldo Emerson

Each of us was brought up with the idea that we have a talent that we are born with, a natural inkling that we are good at. May it be singing, dancing, acting, mathematical and spatial intelligence or even discrete skills like fine motor movements, mostly become evident at a very young age.

Whether it is purely genetic, a subconscious influence or an upfront persuasion from the parents to their young, children eventually grow up into adults that seem to lead an invisible paved path towards something close to their "natural talents". Although it is not all the time that everything goes well as planned, given the various circumstances like parental preference, financial capacity, and other factors, adolescents usually can already identify where they are good at and the things they would like to pursue. Aside from the other uncontrollable factors, there is a tragedy in our current societal structure, and that is its rigidity in promoting focus in only one field. Wherein, the trend now is *specialization* and *subspecialisation* and even *sub-subspecialisation*.

People who are engaged in multiple fields that are unrelated are sometimes frowned upon or discouraged, referring to them as "Jack of all trades, master of none". Honestly, while growing up, I am guilty of feeling inferior and confused by liking so many things all at once and cannot pinpoint which among many things I love the most. It is only recently that I have come across an episode of TED Talk which appeased my heart. It talked about people being ***multi-potentiated***, and how the most remarkable occurrences in human history are made by the exact people who engaged in different fields and merging the knowledge they have from those fields to come up with something that is actually great enough to leave a mark in history. Like *Leonardo Da Vinci* – a polymath who was also an inventor, musician, architect, and scientist; *Albert Einstein* – a genius who influenced practically all of modern physics and philosophy of science; *Michelangelo* – an Italian sculptor who is also an architect and a poet; and many more, they went against the common notion that people are naturally *left-brained* or *right-brained*.

You see, it is true that there is never an equal balance between one's creativity (right brain) and logic (left brain). By at least a point or two, a person is most likely inclined to be a little bit more rational, orderly objective, symbolic, analytical and strategic than imaginative, artistic, intuitive, emotional and instinctive, or the other way around. However, it should not become conclusive that one will only prioritize that side of the brain and completely eliminate the other.

That is exactly what *potentials* are and not utilizing them might lead to *disuse* and eventually, may die off.

The true capacity of our brain is limitless with the right amount of stimulation, correct practice and application. Thus, reaching an expert level in multiple areas of your brain is actually possible. Remember, our *brain* is now considered to have its greatest power attributed to *plasticity*. Meaning, it has unlimited capacity in adapting to any degree of challenges with the right amount of acceleration. And on average, it is said that we only utilize only a meager percentage of our brains. Thus, the more you use your brain, the better it actually gets.

On a personal note, I would like to consider myself lucky for being born from a mother who is very optimistic, patient and child-friendly. Growing up, I absorb everything around me. The first career path I expressed on liking is being a policeman, then a teacher, then a painter. Another day I would love to be a scientist and an architect and an engineer the next. And each dream is welcomed with open arms, no questions asked. And it is not because we have the means to do it, but simply because of my mother's optimism of an unknown future and her sheer incapacity *to hurt* a young child's heart. I would draw anything and when I showed it to her; she would make a check mark and put *100/100* on it, signifying a perfect score. Sometimes it's 99 and she will point out the area where I could improve. As a result, it boosted my confidence to a point that when I showed my drawings to my playmates, they laughed and told me it's rubbish. However, I was not affected at all. Because deep within me, I just thought *"they are just children who don't know what a good drawing looks like, but my mother knows best, and it is her judgment that I believed in."* Later I knew my drawings were really awful. But, good thing it was already too late to cause me damage. Because when I learned about it, I was already in high school and already practiced well enough to be chosen to represent my class on a charcoal portrait painting contest and regional mural contest. And currently, I accept commissions for all kinds of artworks, while at the same time working full time as a physician who also does baking, professional make-up, photography, sewing clothes/dressmaking, terrarium building, and yes, writing.

Pardon the self-indulgence there, but the main point of that story is to show how potentials are there for everyone. It just needs to be cultivated the right way.

Yes, there are greater opportunities when potentials are yielded at a young age. But do not fret if you are no longer on your teens because no one is too old to learn anything and become a master at it. An old dog can always learn a new trick given that the same dog is also open-minded and is willing to go through the necessary work. In fact, my mother, who is almost 65 years old, is already halfway on her baking class this week.

Unlike others who have glaring talents, I always consider myself as having none in terms of those that can be presented during "talent show portion" or the ones in stage contests. Maybe like me, you might also think that you have none as well. But recently, after constant self-reflection and meditation, I have come to acknowledge the things that I can do that are actually worthwhile, the potentials that I have, and the multi-potentials that I can maximize, but used to disregard. And fully acknowledging such, is also what I want for you to do; because I know you have multi-potentials too.

Knowing and realizing your own multi-potential is very important because it is the only way that one can achieve life's fulfillment. Through implementation and practical application, these multi-potentials can help one cope with whatever stressor he or she is facing. From emotional struggles to even financial limitations, pinpointing your multi-potentials can provide you the solutions you never could have imagined.

If you are ready, get a pen and answer the following questions thoroughly to uncover your multi-potential and at the same time enjoy this life.

1. Which field of practice do you have the most experience with? *It can be your profession, vocation or anything that you've done for the longest time.* It doesn't need to be fancy. It could be your current job or the degree you've obtained or it can be as simple as keeping a tidy room or cooking for your family or raising children or being a great friend can already be counted. You can even be as specific as to what type of food you have perfected all these times.

2. What kind of help do other people often ask you to?

3. What is the activity that you do that gives you the most happiness and a sense of fulfillment?

4. Try to think of the compliments you frequently receive. Where do they usually directed? What kind of compliments do you usually receive? *Note that these*

compliments may be something that you do not pay attention to.

5. What are the things that you feel you can consider doing for the rest of your life?

After answering these questions, take a moment and ponder upon them. And see which of these you can hone and practice more. You can rank them by preference and then you can make priorities as to which of them you'd like to master first, or do simultaneously. Trust that you can do it. And please do not limit yourself by the education you got from school because it is only a meager portion of what your true potentials are. Education is best attained in the real world, where you practice it and apply it as you wish.

If at this point you are still unsure, you can try the "Passion Recipe" by Steven Kotler. This is where you make a list of 25 things you are interested in or simply curious at. It could be any topic, skill or knowledge you'd always wondered about. And then, try to make connections. Lump 3-5 of those on your list and make a connection, on how you can collaborate them into one activity. *For example, I was always interested in baking, care of cactus and succulents and healthy meals eating low-carbohydrate foods. To mix them all, I can try to bake a low-carb cake and cupcakes with frosting and designs like cactus and succulent.* Then, dedicate at least 10-15 minutes each day dedicated to research or readings regarding that topic until you get a good grasp of it. This way, a simple list of curiosity can garner more interest that can be turned into your own passion. Take a moment of your own. Pause and write that Passion Recipe now if you wish.

Note that after you establish your Passion Recipe, it is important for you to dedicate time on it. Include a good 10-15 minutes during your personal growth time daily to improve your knowledge or skill related to that list of interests. Doing so will fuel these interests and curiosities to become a passion and not just fade away like those spur of the moment object that once crossed your mind.

Living in this modern era, we should maximize the technology that we can utilize to advance our talents. With many tutorial videos that can provide you with basic and even expert tips and tricks, with time and effort, you can be one yourself. And you may say that time is a hindrance. But I do not believe it. If you feel you are not yet at your best self, then most likely, you are engaging in activities that are actually not enriching your personal growth. Sometimes, it is already embedded in our routines that we miss to see it. It can be as innocent as unmindful watching on TV or movies, browsing through social media, reading fiction or engaging in small talks, or playing games that don't add value to your person. If you can identify what you can eliminate in your day and replace it with an activity that can boost your potential, then you are on your way to fully tap them.

According to Pareto Principle, most, if not all in our life is guided by 80/20 rule. This means that 80% of your actual productivity or *the needle-moving activities* are done in 20% of your effort and time. On a larger scale, 80% of a company's revenue is actually made by only 20% of all of the employees. Thus, if you can identify what are the 20% tasks that are producing 80% of your outcome in a day to day basis, you can replace other non-essential tasks with more *needle-moving* ones.

So, how about if you have regular work and you are living far from your work and a lot of your time is spent on the road, worse, in traffic? The good news is, you can make the most of this time by listening (*if you are driving*) to informative podcasts and audio books or watching (*if you are just a passenger*) videos and documentaries that can help you with the improvisation of your knowledge and skills. This is what we call "*Bus University*", "*Walking School*" or "*Train College*". In the Philippines, it can be a "*Taxi Course*" or a "*Jeepney Masterclass*". Well, you get it. The important part here is for you to make the most of your time and be mindful of your own strengths and weaknesses so you can awaken all of the potentials that you have to fully live this life.

Before we end this chapter, note that this is no call for simply multi-tasking. But, it is a call for you to maximize the time that you have. By knowing your potential, and as you master your craft, you will be able to beautifully stratify your day in the most productive way. At first you might get overwhelmed. That is why it is important for you to take time in self-reflection, because that is where you will develop your intuition in adequately managing your day. Allot a certain time for important facets in your life like work/finances, personal development, and important relationships while incorporating mastery of your multi-potentials. None of it must be jeopardized because you have the power to succeed in all of these aspects. If you apply the Pareto principle, your job/current state now occupies 20%. You can take another 20% for personal growth time, another 20% for your loved-ones and relationships, 20% for reflection, spiritual allocation, meditation or journaling and the last 20% for your personal effects or can be spent in in sharpening the saw of your current craft to double your productivity or an activity that is productive and enjoyable at the same time. It may sound like a full schedule, but it is the most satisfying and gratifying one.

This way, you will not be overwhelmed nor even appear to be busy. Because you will be operating in an extraordinary and efficient way, every task is well calculated thus appear effortless, but needle-moving. You remain calm yet steadfast and people will only wonder how you are able to do so many things that you do given that you are living in the same 24-hour daily realm. Surprise them. But most importantly, surprise yourself.

This is simply one of the many things you can do as you embrace the inner calm within you, no matter what chaos is around.

CHAPTER IX

Third, Offer Yourself to What is Good without Expectation

"Then give to the world the best you have. And the best will come back to you."

Madeline Bridges

Once you have identified and tapped your multiple-potentials, it is then best to offer these gifts to the world. These potentials are truly precious when it is intrinsically good and when developing it can help the life of others it can come in contact with.

Remember the passion recipe the previous chapter? We can further advance that by thinking about a problem that is currently being faced by people in the world and try to think how your passion can address that problem. To make your passion the answer to a problem can lead to purpose. This is the PPP Happy Formula:

Problem + Passion as a Solution = Purpose

Take for example, my mother's top 5 problems she wants to see solved include ending war, poverty, drug addiction, gambling & women's oppression. While her interests include travel, learning something new, helping people, listening to radio, singing and spending time with loved-ones. This passion list may seem far out, but there is actually a way to make it into an answer.

She can spend time learning all things while *listening to the radio*, anything that is related to, say for example, *drug addiction*. Once she has garnered a full knowledge about drug addiction and how it can be prevented or addressed, she can *share it with her loved-ones while spending time with them*. And when she *travels*, she can go to the community leader to gather people and she can share her knowledge about it. She can even write a song or just find a song that supports this cause and *sing it*. This way, she is living her passion while also providing a solution for a problem she want to resolve.

You see, there is a way for any passion to become an answer to any problem. You just have to open your heart and be creative on how you can do it. Know your purpose, ask from your heart "what would it take for me to accomplish it" and the answer will be provided.

Yes, this is very much doable. But I admit, for some, this becomes tricky and can even be the greatest source of stress. You can think of something that you do that didn't turn out the way you wanted or my mother not seeing drug addiction ending. Like an artist that after creating a masterpiece, fell on misery when he didn't get the attention he had pictured out. This stress or disappointment is understandable when knowing your own worth somewhat automatically equates to expecting the same recognition and affirmation from the world. But when what you do doesn't pay off with your expected outcome, then this dissonance is the spark that can easily lead to a total fire of self-doubt, anxiety and even depression.

I also have found myself in this kind of situation in the past. And it is only recently that I have recognized what's been missing all along. The answer is in the first paragraph, the same idea I have known since ethics class more than 10 years ago: the key concept here is "***intrinsically good***". You see, when what you do is genuine, kind and good on its own, then you have to recognize it as the ***end goal*** in itself and NOT the means towards another end. Being able to do it is already the reward in itself. Gather all positivity and be grateful that you have done it. The rest, whether with recognition or not from the external world, is no longer part of the definition of being fulfilled.

To put it in another perspective, *my mother*, not seeing the complete resolution of drug addiction despite the fact she did her best in trying to end it, should already be at peace knowing that she took part and gave it her all. Whatever the outcome of her effort is already beyond her control, but *her effort alone* that is *intrinsically good*, is already *a goal achieved,* with or without external affirmation. And as for the artist, he should focus and remember on why he created that masterpiece in the first place. The fact that he enjoyed every stroke and he embraced every line he created from start to finish with the intent of letting the audience feel the emotions he felt, as *to provide a means of expression of what others cannot express in words*, is already an end goal and a success on its own.

Sure, in this modern world, everything seems to have a different tangible yardstick, and most often it is monetary, while for others, it is fame and attention. But the artist must remember that having those as the ultimate outcome is bound to create only heartaches and disappointment. Not only because those things are beyond one's internal control, but most importantly, it drives the artist away from the main reason why he is doing the things that he does in the first place and that act alone is already the goal being accomplished.

Thus, when the artist focuses only on the intrinsic goodness of his masterpiece, then completing it is already enough. The mere completion becomes a source of satisfaction and the outcome from an external measure of success becomes insignificant especially in causing stress.

This principle is one of the core learning I've had in my adult life. However, at some time, I also got confused. From little appreciation and good words from others, those words slowly build up to a point that I have put importance to the external value of what I do. It took some time for me to realize that indeed I have lost focus. After some reflection, things became clearer, and I decided to start again. But this time, with the perspective of doing my best with the purest intention of helping others live better, and whether it will actually happen or not, it is already beyond me. Doing my part to my very best is already enough, and this made all the difference. The stress went away the moment I no longer have expectations, and it is now inner peace, more than happiness, filled my soul.

Do not get me wrong. I am not saying that you will ignore the external outcome that your own masterpiece will have. You will still recognize it and use it to your advantage without disrupting your inner peace. By considering the good comments and praises, you can take it as a bonus, like a cherry on top and an opportunity to express *gratitude*. Always give thanks no matter what. And when negative feedbacks are in place, take it as an opportunity to improve. It takes practice, but you can learn to be open to it and go back to your core goal to do well. And there is no better way to do it than keep on improving.

In this world of social media, even a certain Facebook post that doesn't get enough likes and comments can be a source of one's disappointment. This is because the majority lost focus on the reason why they post it in the first place. The number of likes and comments becomes the source of joy and the mode of measurement of their success. But if you really look closely, say for example a photo that you personally like because looking at it made you feel good, you share it in hope that others who can see it can feel good as well. Then, the mere posting of that photo becomes *the end*, should already be enough regardless of the number of like shares or comments that you get.

As of this point, try to think about what is it that you do best that you can offer to the world? What is its purpose? What is its genuine and intrinsic goal? Note that most gifts do not have an obvious impact, but know that it has. Below are the examples you can gauge your own talent on:

- Engineers create things that make life easier.

- Architects make a safe and beautiful structure to work or live in.

- Teachers improve the future by helping children learn.

- Artist improves lives by making each moment better through a painting, a poem, a dress or a song. Or by providing the means of expression of feelings people cannot make words for.

- Salespersons bridge the gap between producers and buyers.

- Assistants and Secretaries contribute largely to the cause that their employers do. Without them, success can be endangered.

- Parents rear children that can become responsible citizens in the future.

- Priests and other spiritual leaders provide peace and reassurance.

- Businessmen provide services that customers need.

Those examples mentioned and many more, have intrinsic values of their own. By knowing what you can do, how you can do it best and finally doing it in hopes of bettering your situation and that of others, you are already living your purpose.

Know your own value more, recognize it, cultivate it and offer it to the world. Make the offering as the *"end"*- the ultimate goal. Be happy with it alone and nothing else can break that because it is yours and yours alone for the taking.

Be happy, you deserve to always be.

SECTION 4

Overcoming Personal Struggles

"To be aware of a single shortcoming within oneself is more useful than to be aware of a thousand in somebody else"

XIV Dalai Lama of Tibet

CHAPTER X

Self-doubt

"The only person you are destined to become, is the person you decide to be"

Ralph Waldo Emerson

Only you can do the things you do. Self-doubt is a poison that can benefit no one, and worse, it can jeopardize the most important entity there is, and that is you.

Let go of your worries. Our mind is more powerful than we can ever imagine. As *Henry Ford* said, whatever you choose to believe becomes the reality. For sure you have had your own fair share of experiences wherein your thoughts become reality. Unfortunately, we as humans do not maximize this great power that we have. Instead, we succumb to pessimism and negativity and eventually lead to keep repeating the same fate. In psychology, it is a defense mechanism called *"brace for loss effect"*, that is when one prepares himself for the worst-case scenario so that any other outcome, even if the worst one, becomes easier to accept and deal with. I, myself, have been guilty of such. And although it may seem beneficial at a quick glance, this strategy actually has a big drawback. That is, one is more likely to attract the negative outcome to manifest more than the best one.

So, how can we battle such self-doubt? Is it as simple as not considering the worst outcome and just always imagine the best results without a back-up plan? Or can we have it both ways and maximize it to our advantage? Fortunately, the latter can be done.

You see, *self-doubt* is not there for nothing. In fact, it is a core human trait that enabled our race to survive this long. In a way, self-doubt is protective because it will enable us to prepare ahead when things go sideways. It is embedded in our amphibian brain to be wary and anxious, so as to anticipate the potential undesirable results. Thus, the *first step* in dealing with self-doubt is to **embrace** it, come face to face and deal with it firsthand. Consider self-doubt as an *intuition* or as a *devil's advocate* to look into "*you*" one more time. Be realistic and objective. Be your own first critic. Because if you feel that there is self-doubt, then most likely, there is actually something that can be improved. Thus, go and scrutinize each step. Whether it is a personal project or involving others, take the parts that you can improve on your own and do everything that you can do to make it better. Go over it as many times as you can, as many times as needed and as many times you are allowed.

Once you are satisfied, you can proceed with the *second phase* of foreseeing the worst possible outcome that is beyond your control and **prepare** for it, by fully accepting it should it happen and by making a Plan B or making the most of what can be done after. Do this second step in a jiffy and not a minute more. This way, you are ready for anything yet not be consumed with fear.

And finally, savor this *last step* by taking your time. Differing from the previous two steps, in this phase, you vividly **visualize the best possible outcomes** that there could be and have as many great possibilities that you can think of, regardless of the overwhelming odds against it. Best, think of the most ideal outcome. Close your eyes and rank these possibilities and focus on the feeling of positivity as if that outcome has already happened, notwithstanding the odds. Savor that sense of fulfillment and satisfaction and be grateful for that best result. Linger on that goodness and be grateful for it. This way, you are increasing your chances of succeeding by attracting what is good and by welcoming a beautiful outcome. Then, finish it all with a sense of peace knowing that you got everything covered.

These simple three steps comprise a fail-proof plan because it will make you prepared for anything, and more importantly, you are enabling positivity to come into alignment with whatever that is in your heart.

Should it still persist, think of how far you've already come. As humans, we sometimes tend to forget the bad things that happened to us and the struggles that we have faced in the past simply because the memory might give you an unpleasant reminder. But you can look at those experiences from a different angle. Look at it as a trophy that you have surpassed and succeeded. And upon recognizing a lot of obstacles you have conquered, any task at hand surely becomes manageable. This is what they call as a *reverse gap*. It is the gap between where you are now and where you have been in past 5 or 10 years ago. Whether it is physical improvement, monetary, progression of a skill set or a simple new mentality or better mind set, for sure you have come a long way. Entrust to a higher being and have faith that you have been guided an invisible hand in the past and you will still be guided to do what is right.

In addition, as emphasized with the previous chapter, just do what you do best, do it with all of your compassion and nothing else will matter.

Bear in mind the intrinsic goodness of an act and the kindness that your duty has, by doing it to the best of your knowledge and intention. There is no point lingering in self-doubt. The time you spend thinking about it is counterproductive, thus, it is better to use that time improving your craft instead. That way, you improve yourself and eventually improve your own overall sense of satisfaction. And finally, you will be on your way to achieving all the things that matter to you the most.

CHAPTER XI

Childhood and Adult Trauma

*"Your well-being affects (and is affected by)
those waves through small ripples of self-care
and the decisions you make."*

Melissa Steginus

The worst part of abuse and trauma is the fact that approximately 90% of it is perpetuated by people known by the victim, which, sadly, would include family members and other acquaintances. Strangers, the kind that we often warn our children to be wary about just comprise less than 10% of the overall statistics of actually causing the abuse and the eventual trauma to the growing child. Abuse and trauma can be inflicted in many forms. It can range from a barely-there incident like an unconscious mean comment, or it can be as harsh as physical abuse leaving both palpable and invisible scars. As evolving humans, children grow up with these experiences, and when left un-*dealt* with, can shape them up into the person that may not be the best version of themselves. Personally, I have my own share of unpleasant experiences. And although I overcame and persevere over time, I know too well that the same may not be processed as swiftly by others, if at all. Regardless of the specific cause of trauma, no one has the right to quantify which trauma is more severe than the other because *perception*, just like in many things, is relative. But for the young mind, no bad experience is too small to ignore. If you are a victim of such, in any way, the first thing that you can do is recognize that as a child, even if how mature you thought you already were, then, you were still too young to protect yourself from your source of trauma or stress. More importantly, you were still too young to guard yourself against your own destructive thoughts. Thus, you can let go of it by accepting the past as it is, and as something that cannot be undone. However, this time, do not let that unpleasant experience define the person that you are now.

I know that as a child, we have the tendency to blame things to our parents or our guardians, but as the adult that you are now, no matter how hard it may seem, we have to let go of that tendency. I know that some of us literally deserve better parents, while others were blessed to have parents who helped them recover as soon as they were injured. But for those who grew up like they were raising themselves, it is high time for you to actually give yourself a *pat on the back* and talk to your younger self, declaring how proud you are of him/her, for surviving and thriving amidst all the things that you've been through. It has been suggested that one way to deal with it is to revisit the inner child within you, and becoming the parent to that young version of you, which can sometimes become the healing that one needs. It is what they call *"parenting your inner child"*. Because the trauma may not be your fault, but the process of healing is your responsibility. You owe yourself that. You deserve that.

You can take a pause right at this moment and recall your own experiences. You may close your eyes if necessary. Imagine the young you, sitting right in front of you. And take this moment to talk to that younger version of yourself, assure him/her that he/she will get over it and that he/she will survive it all and more importantly, that it will only get better from this day on. Say these words to the scarred child within you:

"You are strong. You are brave. You are amazing. You have survived. You can thrive. It is not your fault. I am proud of you. It is going to be okay. We will be okay. We are okay."

Repeat these words ten times or as often as necessary and you may add more if you wish. Accept that you are not to blame. Know that whatever it is that you have experienced, it is no longer true now. You are now all grown up. You are now in control. May it be physical, emotional or mental trauma, those things can no longer affect you the same way it did before. Heal yourself by forgiving the past, accepting it as a mere moment that passed and look at it as an obstacle that you have successfully surpassed, and start anew with a sense of control of your own life.

Learn that skill. Visit that magical place. Transform yourself to the person you always wanted to become. And for those who were deprived of opportunities growing up, it is now time that you grant yourself those healthy indulgences the moment you can already afford it. This is where you can apply one of my life's favorite mantra: *If the world cannot give to me, then, I will give it to myself.*

And as for traumas other than childhood, it can also happen in adulthood as well. And we may not want to admit it, but sadly, even adult traumas are said to have patterned from the experiences of the past too. It could be an incident from a personal account or a witnessed trauma during childhood, that one way or another affected one's pattern of trust, distrust and the dynamics in relationships. Note that traumas and phobias do not always happen the way it is portrayed in the movies. Sometimes it can be an innocent comment from a fellow playmate, a nanny or a sibling, someone that you regard as important during that time. An example is a friend of mine who keeps on brushing her hair every chance she gets and eventually we learned that it all started way back when she was still in grade school where a classmate of hers asked if she ever combs her hair because it looks messy. Since then, she never leaves the house without a comb and brushes her hair every chance she gets, like a *security blanket*. This case may seem simple, and good thing it led to something that is not debilitating. But, you can take this time to reflect on your own fears, or anything that makes you feel unpleasant, the ones you think you always have. And then, try to recall when it originated, most likely the memory is there but just suppressed. Make sure that as you do this exercise, you are in a secure place with enough privacy for you to be with your own thoughts. If you feel you are not yet ready, you can skip this part and go back to it as soon as your situation can allow. And when you do, be comfortable with your own consciousness and be the commander of your own thoughts.

Do not be afraid to open it up, because you are safe now and it is necessary for you to open that dark box in order for you to fully move forward and maximize the life that you have today.

As hard as it may seem, mentally envisioning and forgiving the person or the situation that led you to that trauma is more freeing than you will ever know. Forgive them, and then, forgive yourself. I understand that sometimes, we tend to hang on to our heartaches and grudges because this is our own way of giving justice to whatever injustice that we felt we've encountered. For others, these "injustices" are not even perceived consciously, but it can manifest as a perpetually suppressed negative feeling toward another person that one may not be able to identify where it originated. But once recognized your journey towards healing can finally ensue.

Given that you already know how intrinsically complicated human life is, it may seem challenging, but we can **have the heart** even for those who caused us pain. Perhaps, they themselves were also going through the same internal chaos, and in the process of trying their best to stay afloat at that given moment, they unconsciously caused waves of struggles to another, including us.

There can be two ways to go about it. As someone advocating internal locus of control, I have a personal inclination of wanting to see justice being served, or better yet, being a part of that entity that made justice happen. However, this can be delicate because it carries a degree of negativity that a person may invisibly hurdle. One way to do it is through *de-personalization*. This is where you forgive the person internally, making him/her no longer a source of threat and pain, and at the same time does not provide them the opportunity to repeat the same offenses again. One of the most common techniques is through *escape and avoidance*. And pairing it up with peace of internal forgiveness, this could be enough justice for most.

The other way to do it is to openly forgive the person, and entrusting everything to a higher power, that in one way or another, justice will be served. Letting go of what has been and plainly moving forward (*even with the offender still a part of your active life*) is a gift that you might have. This strategy has been the most suggested approach by professionals and counselors alike and is actually the most liberating way. Practicing this craft of forgiveness in any situation in your life will lead to a more positive outlook. Even minor encounters like another car cutting you on the road. Having a mantra of *"I forgive you and I hope you forgive me too"* can do more good to your internal milieu than any other form of anger management tactics that there may be because this line comes from a place of kindness, the genuine and sincere kind. You may think you are at a disadvantage, but the peace, positivity, and healing that comes with it are surely worth it.

Whatever strategy you decide now, acknowledge that this time, the power is in your hands. No one else, but you, is in control *of you*.

CHAPTER XII

Repeated Failures

"Success is not final, failure is not fatal: it is the courage to continue that counts."

Winston Churchill

As discussed in chapter V, repeated failures are potential areas of improvement. And in order to do so, one must recognize such a recurring pattern and accept the fact that something must be done. Once acceptance is covered, then, appropriate intervention can follow.

The first on the list is to forgive yourself with the failures of the past. Just like in traumas and previous experiences, what happened before cannot be undone, but for you to let it happen again is a totally different story, if not plain *absurdity*. Thus, simply put, forgiving yourself has an accompanying promise for you to consciously try to do better next time, if not totally avoid it.

Secondly, proceed with analyzing each scenario and thoroughly consider what went wrong and where you could possibly improve it. No matter what kind of experience you wish to progress, there is always a window of opportunity for you to do it better. As a practice, you can try to recall any big or small unpleasant scenario you've had for the last 24-48 hours and try to imagine, what you could have done, to make it have a better outcome. Remember to not put the blame on others, but take control of the situation and maximize whatever you think you can do to transform that incident into a positive one. Once established, make a necessary plan of action on how will you address each lapse that you had, and how you can avoid it the next time around.

Lastly, be mindful of the situation. Develop foresight in order for you to see if you are about to face the same or similar situations again. And then this time, implement the plan of action you have previously established. Deliberately stir away from the same decision that led you to have that repeated failure in the first place. Take a step back if necessary for you to fully see the bigger picture. Take a deep breath and trust that this time, you are doing it better. It may take some practice, but once mastered, this can become a bullet-proof approach so long as you maintain honesty and objectivity during your analysis of the situation.

Take responsibility for the things that you did no matter how wrong it is and let go of the circumstances that were beyond your control while at the same time deliberately maneuvering the aspects that you can run without stepping into another person's freedom to exercise the same.

CHAPTER XIII

Addictive Behavior

"One of the hardest things was learning that I was worth recovery."

Demi Lovato

Addiction is defined as anything that a person engages in uncontrollably despite the risk of such behavior towards self and others, loved ones and work included. To distinguish it from other forms of compulsive acts, addictive behaviors are those that are done by individuals despite the overt and expected untoward outcomes. The most common forms of addiction include alcoholism, illicit drug-use, those that involve sexual acts, smoking, and gambling. Some less popular, but also damaging forms include online gaming, shopping, hoarding, eating sugary foods, and other activities that usually started as a remedy to stress.

However, over time, this supposedly temporary remedy gave the needed shift away from stress, to a totally opposite feeling of elation that it becomes too hard for the person to let go.

Common stories would include a student or a worker who cannot seem to finish his necessary tasks within the day. As an instant fix, he took some stimulant drugs to keep him awake and active. And true enough, it succeeded. He was able to finish his work without feeling tired despite not having enough sleep. For the lucky few, they go back to their previous routine as if it didn't happen. But then the next project comes, and you know what comes to mind? Yes, it is the stimulant that he once tasted so good it left a very strong and shortened pathway right on his consciousness. Thus, on average, a person who has tried it, cannot help but think about it. And without will power and enough motivation to say "No", it could be a start of a vicious cycle of a person's addictive behavior.

Another startup story would be someone who has been in pain, either literally from a physical injury or emotional pain, like the pain caused by the loss of a loved one. These pains are sometimes too much to bear that they needed help from external and often, chemical forms to alleviate such hurt. Starting from a few tablets of ibuprofen to stronger relaxants, it can escalate to *opioids*, also known as narcotic drugs that are either controlled, regulated and sometimes, illegal like *heroin*.

It may sound a little scary, but do not be afraid if you haven't been on this road. Studies have shown that addictive behavior is partly genetics, wherein one's tendency to have it is actually written in their genes. Thus, if you are one of the lucky ones, stresses are managed by many defense mechanisms not involving addictive behaviors, my favorite of which is *sleeping* or just taking a rest, or a break from the rest of the world.

If you belong to those who are far from possibly engaging in any addictive behaviors as a form of de-stressing, the idea of using such substances is minimal. However, for those who have been on that road, it actually doesn't appear that "*off*" for them. Contrary to common belief, those diagnosed with addiction or substance abuse, mostly did not show any intellectual inferiority compared to people who didn't. Meaning, it does not follow that an addict is less intelligent than the ones who don't have any addictive tendencies. In fact, some even have superior intelligence and tried these illicit drugs thinking that they are "smart enough" to be able to control it. Some even take it as a challenge to prove to others that they are the ones controlling it, proving themselves above than those who are already damaged by drugs. Unfortunately, many end up trapped in that vicious cycle and can succumb to a lifelong addiction or even early demise if not intervened early on.

As of this point, you might ask, how can we avoid such addictive behaviors? And for those who are already suffering from it, is there still a way to save them? Is there hope to save you or me?

I want to assure you that, yes; the hope is big enough to cover everyone. And as a reminder, whether you believe you can or cannot, you are right. So, better believe you can as early as now.

To start this journey towards addiction reversal, one must first recognize that there are two important circuits in the brain that we need to look into 1) *Pleasure Center* and 2) *Satiety/Satisfaction Center*.

As discussed in the earlier part of this book, the **pleasure center** is the one that is activated by drugs, sugary foods, gambling, and the likes. These activities do not activate the satiety or **satisfaction center**, thus the person has an insatiable appetite to keep on engaging in those activities despite the fact that it already jeopardizes everything else. Instead, a person suffering from an addictive tendencies can choose to engage in other form of activities that are productive and enjoyable. Examples are activities that can give the sense of satisfaction and at the same time, have some degree of pleasure to counter the previous maladaptive behavior. This is where a person's interests, likes and people in his life must corroborate in helping him move towards a more beneficial activities. It may be challenging at first, but acknowledge the millions who have recovered that are also living testaments that it can be done.

Knowing this fact can help one acknowledge why they almost cannot stop themselves from doing it. But believe that it can be stopped and it will. As they say, *if you can stop it once, you can do it for a lifetime.*

There are many approaches to weaning or the practice of withdrawal from those addictive activities. Some consider a slow withdrawal while others do it abruptly. But when you are truly decided to do it, then a *one-time big-time all-or-none approach* must be taken. Remember, the more you take, the more you crave. Thus, it may be hardest during the first few days, but with persistence, it can lead to faster adaptation of not craving for it even more.

In each instance that there is a craving, try to take salt. It may sound absurd, but studies show that it has value in reducing any form of cravings. Salt is the most abundant and essential electrolyte and the fastest to be depleted as well. Research shows that those with adequate and unrestricted salt intake among test subjects showed less tendency for addiction than those with a lowered salt intake. This is because our body is very adapted to high salt intake and not to low salt intake, as advocated by most. Thus, when one has low salt in their system, the brain senses this inadequacy and fills it up with the experience that gave it the "high" that it has the most significant memory. And sadly, these are the experiences that are unrelated, even far out, but provide an insatiable pleasure instead, *just like when one won in gambling, the sweetness of sugary foods, or the euphoria from illicit drugs, or alcohol.* That pleasurable memory dominates the person's mind, and wrongly attributing the need for salt and other nutrients to those activities facilitate addictive behavior.

Truth be told, I know that I, too, have addictive genes within me. We came from a family of gamblers and voracious eaters. Thus, by the time

I reach 20, I have decided I will no longer play any games on my gadgets because I know for sure I will get easily addicted if I start one. Also, as someone advocating mindfulness, it has been my personal rule to always be in control of my own thoughts. This is the reason why I do not drink alcoholic beverages nor take medicines or any substance that can chemically alter my brain function, especially if it can jeopardize my call of judgment. It may sound rigid for some, but I believe that this is the only way for me to truly live, and stay in touch with reality to its very core.

(Note though that I do not impose this "No alcohol rule" to anyone. I am almost always present in many important gatherings of family and friends with some alcoholic beverages involved. I have fun with them all night and can even join the fun the same way they would, except that I am my 100% sober self. Also, I am most grateful for the people in my life respecting my decision without pressuring me to do anything I do not want to.)

For those who would like to recover from addiction, the following tips may be considered:

1. Acknowledge an addictive behavior.

2. Make a list of reasons and inspiration why you need to be sober.

3. Inform the people who matter about your situation and your willingness to recover.

4. Do self-inspection and revisit your past, and examine where and what triggered that addiction in the first place.

5. Just like in trauma, forgive and heal yourself.

6. Believe that you deserve better.

7. Establish a new routine wherein you design it in a way that you avoid temptations, including the people and things that might trigger you to engage in it again.

8. Consider that engaging in such behavior will become like food to a *"parasite"* that's

been living inside you, right in your *pleasure center.* Whenever you give in to it, you are feeding it, letting it grow, and the pleasure it gives you is just temporary and superficial so that it can enslave you for long.

9. Have an anchor for you to keep your path straight. It can be anyone, like a loved one, or a spiritual counselor, or it can be your faith or your higher consciousness.

10. Develop an alternative list of activities that you enjoy doing and you can engage in.

11. Have a plan for the future.

12. Make the road towards recovery a commitment to yourself. Treat it as the attention and love that you have deprived yourself for the longest time.

13. Last but not least, do not hesitate to ask for professional help. It is always good to seek one.

CHAPTER XIV

Depression

"Even in the midst of devastation, something within us always points the way to freedom"

Sharon Salzberg

It is said that depression is like an invisible dark cloud hovering above you, or a very heavy sack of burden one carries around on their backs. Some say, those who have it actually have it at all times, but they just learned to act as if it is not there. And unless fully recognized and dealt with, it can stay for as long as the person lives, affecting its life's quality and even its length.

In the *Diagnostic and Statistical Manual of Mental Disorders*, depression can be categorized as either major or minor. It is classified as a mood disorder wherein one experiences a depressed mood and/or loss of interest, together with other symptoms in the same two-week period. These other symptoms include significant and unintentional weight loss or weight gain, restlessness or physical/mental slowing down, fatigue or loss of energy nearly every day, inappropriate feelings of guilt or feelings of worthlessness, difficulty to think or inability to concentrate and recurrent thoughts of death or suicidal ideation.

For those who are suffering from these symptoms or if you know anyone who might be suffering from such a condition, it is strongly advised to seek professional help as soon as possible.

For those people who can easily adapt to various uncontrollable changes in life, unexpected and unpleasant turn of events can be managed without resulting in depression. In general, as mentioned in our 10 core values, one can just let go of the things that you cannot control. This means that when faced with an unwanted scenario, it is okay to feel sad or even to cry, but it should not be to a point where one has already stopped living or decides to put an end to his/her own life.

No matter what the cause, it is said that depression occurs when there is an *absence of happiness at the present* moment as well as *absence of hope in the future.* With repeated undesirable events and lack of perceived controllability, one can be in a state of learned helplessness wherein a person simply just gives up. To further understand this, I will share with you one of the saddest experiments done on dogs. To simplify, dogs in one group were put in a cage and an electric shock was introduced. The shock was terminated whenever they press the lever. In the second group, a shock was also introduced, however, it doesn't stop even if they press the lever. This was repeated many times. In a subsequent experiment, the same dogs were placed in a cage with two platforms. Dogs in group one immediately jumped on the other platform when the shock was introduced and goes to the other "safe" platform. However, dogs in group two just lie down and whine when the shock was introduced. They didn't do anything despite seeing the dogs from group one safe in the other platform. This is what ***learned helplessness*** is all about. It is accepting a negative event and not doing anything about it simply because efforts in the past did not give any different desirable outcome. It is the worst kind of learning. And sadly, this is true for some people. And it is said that no amount of threat, reward or demonstration from others can take away such unfortunate state, which explains the high rate of suicides these days even in the younger generations.

However, I refuse to accept that. We are way better than that. We have the most sophisticated brain in the animal kingdom that is more powerful than we could ever imagine. We just need to tap it. In a nutshell, we can always find something to be grateful for despite everything because there always is. Find a reason to be "happy" here and now. After which, visualize a better future and gather all the love you can get, and let these feelings of compassion lift you up, and pray, that what you hope for, or something better, will unfold.

To tackle this fully, note that some forms of depression occur in an instant, some with a known trigger, while some slowly progressed after experiencing chronic stress or repeated failures that led to emotional build-up over time. The following are the common inciting grounds of depression and how we can possibly mentally counter them.

Major (Unpleasant) Life Event

This is a usual trigger. Loss of a job, a project or business or craft, can make someone question his own capacity and purpose as a person. But to counter this, one can pull himself up and take that loss as an opportunity to improve. When open, one can objectively see an area where the scenario can be improved for the better. It could be a new system for the business, a better product or just a better attitude. As long as you do your best, and commit to living and doing to the best of what you do with the purpose that is intrinsically good, then no major life event can drag you down.

Critical Illness

When you or a loved-one was diagnosed with critical illness, it is of no surprise when feelings of despair comes in especially when the situation appears to be hopeless. But just like any other stressor, there is always a way for you to fully maximize the options that you can within your means. Whether it is modern medicine, alternative medicine or both, the fact that you are doing everything that you can do, all other factors considered, and putting your most positive thoughts and prayers in it is already the first big step.

In a movie documentary entitled *Heal*, a study of 1500 patients with end-stage cancers found to have radical remissions (*or a sudden drastic improvement on their condition*) worldwide were included in a study. They found out that they have

9 common denominators and out of these, only three are related to lifestyle changes, while the other 6 are related to positive thinking and grit to continue living. These are as follows:

1. Changing your diet
2. Taking control of your health
3. Following your intuition
4. Using herbs and supplements
5. Releasing suppressed emotions
6. Increasing positive emotions
7. Embracing social support
8. Deepening your spiritual connection
9. Having strong reasons for living

As for the details, it is already beyond the scope of this chapter. For lifestyle change, I personally recommend reading the first two books of this series. And as for the other aspects, kindly read on and try to apply any amount of optimism you can get here and everywhere.

As a takeaway, the ***strength of faith***, whether it's from belief from God, from the chemotherapy, the radiation, the supplements or energy within you, is the main driving force that can change even an unexpected critical course. You can opt to do this and surrender the rest, and live each day meaningfully the best way possible like it is your last.

Loss of a Loved One

Loss of a loved one is commonly attributed to death. But such an effect can also be extended to a broken relationship and marriages. Such devastating events can affect a person's view of the world. As for death, it is something that is certain for all of us. When one dies, the pain usually comes from loved-ones' unpreparedness, from sudden loss or unexpected causes. And the pain has most often come from regret that is buried deep down. The regret of possibly preventing the demise, regret from things undone, or from words left unsaid. Thus, it is advocated to do the best that you can to the people that matter most to you while they are still around as if they can be gone anytime because that is actually a reality that we all have as living individuals, *but we just choose not to think about often.* And as for those who already lost someone with regrets, forgive yourself and remember how that loved one wouldn't want you to feel bad about it. Accept those and learn from them and do whatever it takes to prevent it from happening again to you or to another beloved.

The adjustment that people left behind by the departed is something that needs to be processed, or else, others might not be able to move on. For immediate families, especially spouses who have been together for decades might have a hard time adjusting to the new life without their partners. No matter how hard, we have to accept that this is one thing that we all need to embrace. This is a part of life and we have to live with it.

The one who succeeds in life is not the most intelligent or the most talented, but it is the most resilient. It is the capacities to adapt to changing life events that make a person attain their true purpose. Yes, it is hard when your partner or parent or sibling or a close friend suddenly disappears. But, you must gather all your strength and get inspiration from all the other people who are still here with you, including the memory of your loved one, who surely wants you to be happy. Engage in activities that bring you joy. If you do not know what it is, try different things until you find it.

The very gift of life is life itself. And you can only see its beauty the moment you decide to fully live it.

Depression of Unknown Cause

It may not appear like it, but this is less likely. More often than not, there is usually an organic inciting event that one failed to realize. Sometimes it's the very minute details of day to day life that are perceived negatively (*often unconsciously*) that are being accumulated internally.

Like a sudden rain, a failed exam, a stone on the path or an out of stock item. These are compilations of preventable and unpreventable negative happenings that one was not able to fully attribute to the right source: for those that were not attributed to one´s self, no responsibility and action plan was taken. For those that are beyond one´s control, it is a failure to let it go and not attribute it to anything else. Remember that putting the blame into something external leads to dual injury because it reaffirms the negativity that a certain event has.

Thus, if you think you have it or another person you care about is suffering from it, try to gather support and love from all directions. Get professional help if deemed necessary. But most of all, provide self-love above all else. Marisa Peer, one of the world's most acclaimed psychological healers, suggest to put a big note in the mirror saying "I am enough". This will serve as a daily reminder that you are enough and your life alone is precious.

In a book entitled "Love Yourself like your life depend on it" by Kamal Ravikant, he suggested a daily eye gaze exercise wherein you will look at yourself in the mirror, focus on one eye and vocally say the words "I love you" ten times. It may sound funny, but this act alone will impact you like you wouldn't expect it would. This is because eye-contact is a special means of communication imprinted in us. Social experiments demonstrated that 1-4 minutes of eye-contact with someone without words can lead to feelings of love and empathy. So, imagine having that with yourself on a day to day basis. This is recommended to be done every morning before starting your day.

May that simple exercise, paired with positivity bring you and your loved-ones brighter moments and hopeful vision of the future.

SECTION 5

Putting Order to Extra-personal Turmoil

"No matter where you are in life now, no matter who you are, no matter how old you are – it is never too late to be who you are meant to be."

Esther & Jerry Hicks

CHAPTER XV

Family, All the Good and otherwise

"When all the dust is settled and all the crowds are gone, the things that matter are faith, family and friends."

Barbara Bush

Not every one of us was born in perfect families, in fact, maybe none of us are.

Families are beautiful, especially if the people in it are there genuinely rooting for each other's success, choices, and happiness. For some, most of their family is great, but there will always be those whom, if given the option, we'd rather wish we are not related to.

This is because, no matter how much we are alike genetically, personal differences play so many roles even among identical twins. Thus, you can

138

just imagine how the disparity of those who only have a part of their DNA similar to yours.

My point is, even if we are inclined to somewhat demand certain support or kind of regard from family members, such should actually be considered more of a privilege rather than a given right because of individual differences.

Any good treatment you get from the family should be something to be grateful for, and not be taken lightly, thinking that it is something that is already expected. The same way that if we have relatives that are in any way not in congruence with our own goals, visions, and wavelengths, or worse, in total opposite or even directly contradicting our own, we shouldn't be taking it personally. Know that they too are entitled to their own personal opinion. Whatever their reasons are, respect it and do not let it affect you negatively. Rather, you can use such as motivation to do better. You do not need to feel bad about any of it.

This is a matter of looking at the situation differently. Take control of whatever you can control and remember that people are not part of those that you should control. But what you can control are your behaviors that can influence how others see and treat you, and what your reaction would be to such treatment by others.

I have to make it clear that I am not trying to convince you to alienate yourself with your family, but, treat them like any other human beings without expecting anything from them. Any good they make you feel is something to thank for and anything bad is something to be assessed, whether to consider for you to make changes on your own behavior or simply brush it off if it turned out to be pointless.

Personally, I believe that in order for us to be truly free and happy, we should not depend this freedom and happiness from others. Oftentimes, as part of the *Social Exchange mindset* and our human evolution depending on tribes to survive, we expect others, we do well to, to also do good to us. To get respect from people we respect and to receive praise from people we also look up to. Sadly, no matter how genuine your heart is, this mentality is just the very recipe for getting your heart broken.

Instead, no matter how hard it may seem, we have to do things while consciously not expect anything in return. If you give a favor to your parents or your siblings, do it because of love and genuine care, and not because you might need them to do the same to you in the future. Do it because it is the right thing to do and focus on the happiness you feel upon knowing that you made them happy. Let the act of favor alone be the end reason why you do it. Let this act of goodness be the finale of your deed, and not just a means to something else. If we do this to our family, loved ones and others, we will be on our road to only fulfilling days without unnecessary heartaches and disappointments.

And should you choose to not associate yourself with some members of the clan whom you simply feel is only toxic to your soul, then, by all means, you have all the right as well to free yourself from filial bondage. You do not need to be enslaved by the fact that you are blood-related. Regardless of what others might say, so long you know you have not stepped on any other person's shoe, you are free to choose whom you want to spend your time with. Avoid them if necessary or simply ignore them. Time is precious and you have all the right to blissfully spend it with people who only fuel your love for this life, *blood-related or otherwise*.

CHAPTER XVI

Friends, Keeping it Simple

"Lots of people want to ride with you in the limo, but what you want is someone who will take the bus with you when the limo breaks down."

Oprah Winfrey

Some friendships are built over years of togetherness, like your preschool best bud, your own cousin or your high school teammate. Other friendships are created in an instant, like a shared seat on a bus ride. Truly, each of these bonds we have with our friends was formed uniquely and is utterly different from one another. And as we go through life, we accumulate even more despite not making any conscious effort about it. Even now, it still amazes me how we can create an instant connection with people we just met as if we've been living a parallel life path all these years without knowing each other.

We have friends who are like us and we also have those who are totally opposite, yet we adore them just as much. And as we continue living, it is inevitable that we go on separate ways, sometimes literally leaving some friends behind in one place, but still keeps the bond in your heart.

As they say, the best types of friendship are the ones that need the lowest maintenance. It is considered as low-maintenance friendship when you do not talk for months, or even years, yet you are secure in your heart that when life gets tough, you'll always have them and they will always have you the same way, no obligations, yet with a 100% willingness to go the extra mile when necessary.

Consider yourself lucky if you have these kinds of friendships. That even if you haven't replied to their last message, no explanation is required because you are secured that it is for a good reason, and it is an affirmation of that sense of security when they still explain anyway even if they know they don't have to.

Friends are special because these are the people you chose to become family, not just the ones given to you by virtue of birth. And if such friendships develop amongst families, then it becomes the best bond there is.

On the other hand, over the years, as you have interacted with many people during the course of life, you'll realize that friendship, in the real sense of the word, is not something you can just offer or receive lightly. Over time, you will realize that there are people who might act as if they are offering friendship, but eventually you can see that it is just part of their social exchange antics for others to be of use to them. At this point, I do not want you to develop a *"Mean World Syndrome"* wherein you try to see all the bad in others, but I just wish for you to evaluate your relationship with people, especially those you have mixed feelings with. More often than not, these mixed feelings are your foresight telling you that something might not be right. We have to accept that even if how much love and kindness we are willing to give, there will always be those people who, unfortunately, did not develop well enough to be the same.

Instead, they live in a place of competitiveness, jealousy, and insecurity, and if you are not aware of these tendencies, being the genuine person that you are, you may become the very subject of their meanness.

Honestly, those people need help and if you are able to identify them, and care enough to help them, you can share them this book or some insights that can help them unveil their true potential to become the best version of themselves. At the bare minimum, positively wish that they will be shown with enough number of right experiences that will lead to their growth.

Personally, it is my firm belief that once you have tapped your fullest potential or is on the road to self-discovery, *and* already secured with your own thoughts and identity, those feelings of competitiveness, jealousy and insecurity will all go away.

Alternatively, should you decide to let go of the people whom you have objectively evaluated as mere opportunists and manipulators to their own service, then, by all means, you are free to let them go. There is no need for you to feel sorry for the past or the future that you may have if it will only mean jeopardizing your own wellness. Remember, you do not need that many people in your life. In fact, you already have enough people in your life that you want to spend moments with but cannot do so because of a lack of time. So, ask yourself, why waste it on half-cooked friendships and acquaintances when there are far more deserving people, or even activities worth spending the day with?

Treasure the lifelong friendships you have accumulated over the years. These are the ones that you can keep talking to all day and all night. They add value to your life, not because of their profession or the services they can possibly give you in the future, but their mere existence makes you happy. You know you have that authentic kind of friendship when you are more than willing to do things for them without thinking of anything in return and the knowledge that you have alleviated even just a parcel of their day is already more than enough reward for you. And the most beautiful part of it is that even if you did not think about it, most likely, they are the same way to you.

At the other end of the spectrum, the only thing I find acceptable for you to decide on keeping the others (*half-cooked friends*) in tab, those who are not (*yet*) part of those genuine friendship, is with hope that you can help them, in the most altruistic and selfless kind of way, while fully knowing that it can take so much of you. *Maybe it is your life's calling as way for you to contribute to the betterment of this world by helping them become better persons.* And as per locus of control, should you decide to take this course, there will be no point in making complaints or blames because it is you who fully decided on it and no one else. And if you do so, know that I admire you, and I am wishing you all the best. Yes, you have my full respect, you with the kind, generous and gentle soul!

CHAPTER XVII

Status: ~~Complicated~~ HAPPY

"Very little is needed to make a happy life; it is all within yourself, in your way of thinking"

Marcus Aurelius Antoninus

Whatever your relationship status now, you must accept that it is the best one for you right at this moment. If you have doubts, take a minute or two to think over why you have the status that you have now, either single or in a relationship.

If you are in a relationship, consider the real reasons why you are engaged in such. If your answer will entail something like *"the other person completes you or that he/she is the only one for you to be happy"*, then I am afraid you had it wrong.

Relationships usually start with attraction and compatibility that eventually evolved into love. These qualities may kick-start a couple, but what will make it last entails more than that. At minimum, there should be mutual respect, support and loyalty. And without it, then, being in a relationship may not be the best option. If one only receives disrespect from their partner, abuse and betrayal, then maybe it is about time you consider what you are really worth, because there is nothing more wasteful than losing another better day.

For you to be in a relationship, it shouldn't be because you are not enough to stand alone or that you cannot be completely happy if you are not with your partner, but it should be because you love the other person more than you need them for whatever purpose you think they serve. (*Note that this statement may not be applicable to arrange marriages settled like business agreements, because such setup is actually is.*)

This is why I agree with the argument that we should have *100% self-love* before getting into a relationship. Just imagine if you only have 25% of self-love. And all of a sudden, a person shows up giving you 50%. With that amount, you already feel flattered and elated given that you were given that *"much"* love, like a big "Wow!" Think about it. If you love yourself 100%, you won't need to beg love from others and 50% wouldn't be that impressive anymore. You become enough. And if somebody shows up wanting to be a part of your life, you don't get swayed easily. Yes, a high standard they may say. But it is only because you do not deserve anything less. You know how much you're worth, and it should only be around or more than a hundred.

Moving forward, one can be legally married and even financially reliant on the partner, but they can still retain their identity and their *"wholeness"* separate from the other person whom they are engaged in.

Being the other half in a relationship, you have to be complete on your own as a whole being and the other person is just a partner and not a part and parcel of your identity. You both can have a harmonious, symbiotic and productive relationship, but you should recognize that your own identity is not dependent on the other. Thus, should you be in a relationship, legal or otherwise, towards the same or opposite sex, you have to acknowledge that being in a relationship is only an aspect of your life that you chose to have a partner. You, choosing to have a partner, can be for the purposes of maximized happiness out of love, joyful moments or productivity. But, you must understand, that as a person, you are already intact and whole, with or without the other.

For the single ones, note that in this modern-day world, we no longer need to be with someone in a romantic sense. Love, in the brain, is a byproduct of our hunter-gatherer DNA that wired us to look for a partner in order to survive and reproduce. The very basic of all its goals is to pass on the DNA to the next generations, meaning, to reproduce. Thus, you must recognize that with today's society, technology, and lifestyle advancement, to find a pair is no longer necessary in order for one to live a full and meaningful life.

Passion can be fulfilled with the right mindset while support and inspiration can come from family, friends and even people you do not personally know but look up to. We can derive inspiration basically from anyone and anywhere. Love, other than the ones embedded in our genes, is actually best obtained if it came from your deep within first. Radiate such love of others, to your advocacy and to the community and it becomes sustainable in its truest form.

If you are single and are actively or secretly wishing to have a partner, try to assess first why you want to be in a relationship in the first place. In general, common reasons why people want to be in a relationship include a need for love and belongingness, a need for a partner to progress in life or to have children. Other reasons include perceived convenience, the fulfillment of desires and finding *happiness*. However, these reasons, though may seem to be valid at first, are actually not the best reasons why one should be in a relationship. To tackle it one by one, those reasons, when dealt with head-on, are partly due to individual insecurities and personal undergrowth that is wrongly attributed to not having a partner.

This is because, such a need for safety, security, even healing, and improvement, are all facets that must be addressed on your own and with you, taking responsibility for your own well-being. Wrongly putting all these responsibilities in the hands of another is a recipe for disaster.

Yes, I recognize that there are those relationships that actually improve each other's lives and partly, because, they both matured, learned and healed together. But being an adult who is currently single, one should actually grab this opportunity to develop his/her person without the bias of another being. This way, self-discovery is raw, pure and real.

Make a commitment to be the primary source of love for your own self. Maximize your time being alone, tap your fullest potentials and fill in the entire void that no one can truly fill. Truth be told, in these modern times, everything you need a partner for can be outsourced, but the most important one, can only be found right within us, and that is love.

Lastly, even one's goal of having children can also be reassessed, as to why you truly wanted to have children in the first place? This deserves an ample time of pondering because scientifically, the only explanation why we humans have that "instinctive" drive to look for love in order to procreate is just our genes dictating us to produce more, ensuring the survival of the race. But, let's face it. With the rapid rise of our population in the billions, without adequate support to ensure that each newborn will truly contribute to the wellness of humanity, do we really need more children? Now, do not fret if you already have a child. This is no call to abandon them. This is a call to maximize that opportunity you have in your hands to raise a good citizen that can alleviate suffering and do well in this world. As a parent, having a child could provide the greatest joy of all, something incomparable to anything else in this world.

But for those who still have the option, try to reassess first why you want a child in the first place. Common reasons would be to see how their offspring would look like (*a superficial one*), to have someone to continue their legacy (*this can be anyone worthy, have a protégée early on*) or have someone to look after them when they are old. (*This last reason is actually quite selfish. Instead of having a child designed to be of service to you, why not get a real insurance and retirement plan to cover for your senior years?*)

For some, a noble intention of providing love and care to another being are their reason. However, if such is really the case, why not consider adopting? There are so many abandoned children in orphanages, streets, and even hospitals who are in dire need of parental care, and without it, are more likely bound to have a difficult life ahead.

Should you be one of those who initially wanted to have children of your own, I ask you to reconsider, and think past beyond your genetic predisposition and be one with the whole human race, and decide in a way that you can contribute the best way you can.

To put it in another perspective, it is said the there are three situations where we can derive happiness and fulfillment. It could be from **experience**, *growth* and contribution. Of course, we all know that it can mean differently from person to person. But unless you are fully in tuned with your own being, have maximized your potential and able to share your talents with the world as being a part of something that is great than yourself, those bliss may not be felt all at once. And incidentally, these three are embedded once the person becomes *a parent*, or the so-called ***The Parenting Paradox***. The experience from having another soul needing and loving you unconditionally, the learning you get overtime and the ultimate sense of purpose knowing you've raised a child can be positively overwhelming. And it is an "okay" thing. I just hope and pray that should you have the option to plan things ahead, you can try to do so after you've become fulfilled yourself, as a child of the universe that you are.

In the end, the decision will be yours and it will be a basic human right for you to do so. And should you decide to have a child of your own, I hope that you do it after you have fulfilled your own personal aspirations and potentials. This way, you will most likely be ready and fully committed to becoming the best parent that you could be, in rearing a child of the universe, who will grow to be a dutiful and responsible human being that will become a blessing to each and every one he/she encounters.

With these in mind, I do pray that you have a sense of reassurance and better direction in truly appreciating the status that you have now. Whether you are with someone or with yourself, be sure you are on the right track with the right mindset of wholly appreciating life while having a status that is nothing but genuinely *happy*.

For those who are interested to know more, it is recommended to read it extensively in a book entitled "The One: A Life Handbook for All" by my very own sister, Atty. Jane Catherine C. Rojo.

CHAPTER XVIII

Dynamics in the Workplace

"Change will not come if we wait for some other person or some other time. We are the ones we've been waiting for. We are the change that we seek."

Barack Obama

Whether it is in business dealings or a company you work for, it is inevitable that we get to deal with people who are quite more of a challenge than others. For some, changing the environment or quitting a job is a doable option. But in many cases, circumstances force us to deal with them and must come face to face with, on a day to day basis.

In order for us to have a lighter mood after a day's work, first, we must bear in mind how important work is. If the reason why you work is something noble and has a meaning that is greater than just your person, *like a whole family relying on the income that your work provides*, then take that as a motivation and the primary focus of your job. Get inspiration from the security and happiness that you provide for your loved-ones as a byproduct of your work and try not to mind the unpleasant workmates or people you have to deal with. Just do what you do best and keep on improving.

If you have a hard headed subordinate, call their attention in a constructive way and clearly state how you want things to improve. It is crucial that you make instructions clear and simple and never assume anything. Make it a habit to have open communication to avoid misunderstandings and eventual negative project outcomes.

Rather than mere saying, it is best to show your colleagues the right way to do it. Avoid spending so much time instructing; instead, invest more time in hands-on training and mentorship for those you can guide and help develop.

And if you have an unsupported boss, strive to have the best performance still despite it. As long as you stick to doing what is right and you are making it your best, everything else will eventually fall into place. And if not, then it will no longer matter because you already did the most important part, and that is, *giving it your all.* Studies in social psychology have repeatedly proven time and again that a supportive immediate superior who knows how to put a premium in the contributions of his subordinates greatly affects the employee's overall job satisfaction. And expectedly, the opposite, which is an ungrateful and unappreciative boss (*even if it is just a perceived/subjective assessment*), will likely lead to a dissatisfied worker who will eventually have poorer performance if not addressed. Thus, it is vital for the superior to know when to outwardly show appreciation when indicated. If you happen to be the one in charge of another, words of positivity may just mean the world to them and enough for them to keep going and be motivated to even do better.

On the other hand, if you are an employee who has a boss who is not openly appreciative despite objectively knowing you are doing great, then it is in this situation that you do not gauge your level of job satisfaction based on your perceived appraisal of your boss. Instead, give yourself the needed pat on your back should you feel you deserve it and be secured with your own capacity and the value that you contribute to the company. If anything, make that *no-appreciation-treatment* a motivation to keep on doing a great job. Sooner or later, it will all pay off, sometimes, in ways that might just surprise you. So, always keep a positive attitude no matter what your position is, be the source of positivity and always look for inspiration to do better and strive for excellence always. This way, you will be in a position where you are indispensable and regardless of external appraisal, your internal gauge will provide you with the sense of security and fulfillment that you truly deserve.

Trust that no good deed will ever go to waste. Every good you do will eventually come back to you. One way or another, it will all add up to something great; to which will be revealed on a timing that is so perfect, it is almost *magical*.

SECTION 6

Improving Career, Craft and Abundance Flow

"What you are is what you have been. What you'll be is what you do now."

Buddha

CHAPTER XIX

Choosing the Right Career Path

"Nobody gets to live life backward. Look ahead, that is where your future lies."

Ann Landers

As growing children, we tend to go about our day playing and exploring the world innocently and instinctively. However, beyond our awareness, there are adults who were observing and judging our strengths and weaknesses that later on translate to suggestions that sometimes play a role in how we choose our career. Common examples would be a teacher for a child who is showing fondness in mentoring younger children, a police officer for a fierce disciplinarian, a scientist for someone who loves experimenting, a painter for a child who loves art, and many more.

Whether those suggestions on our possible professions were truly from objective observations, or from biased impositions of adults' (*often our parents'*) own inclinations, are already beyond the scope of this text. But it is undeniable that most of us are in a line of work that had a long history as to why we arrive at it in the first place. Often, its inception can be traced back during the early childhood years.

There are those who are lucky enough that even at their very young age, already showed potentials that were later on realized as if it was a path well paved and easily followed. For example, our eldest brother, who has always been good with numbers and words, as well as in balancing things, earned his master's degree in business administration and no matter how much he tries to stick with admin work, always end up thriving in the fields of sales and marketing. Our sister, who has been seen to always stand firm on what she believes in, even on simple things that concern a child, and has a quick wit to counter strong arguments is now a practicing lawyer. Our other brother who has been fond of scrutinizing, sometimes destroying and then repairing things is now an engineer. Whether it was the power of suggestion, a driven inspiration from a model figure, or the verbalization of an obvious inherent personal inclination, in the end, it no longer matters because they are already happy and confident in their chosen career paths.

You will know that your line of work is suited for you when you feel you are thriving in it, contributing significantly to the company or the cause of your work. And if you cannot imagine doing something else other than the work that you do, then most likely, you are in the right place. If you answered yes to all of these, then you are one of those lucky individuals who ended up right where they truly belong. This way, you can further advance your skills and eventually your career by cultivating more of your capacity in order for you to be the best at what you do.

On the other hand, there are other people whose career potentials are not that precise and obvious. Personally, I am guilty of belonging to this group.

If you ask my mother, she will tell you that while growing up, I have exhausted almost all professions from a policeman, a weapons engineer, a painter, an architect, a scientist, a teacher, an inventor, a veterinarian, a chef, a photographer, a flower arranger, a doctor, a jewelry maker, a counselor, a farmer, and many more (*except for anything that involves sales and money*). And sometimes, these "what I want to be when I grow up"-line would change on a day to day basis depending on what probably inspired me that day in school or in the streets. And I am blessed with a mother, that despite having an actual circumstantial difficulty, never stopped me from dreaming of becoming all those. Because, even if not having a definite inclination might appear disadvantageous at first glance, with proper support and motivation, it could lead to something that is even more beautiful.

You see, we were brought up in such a way that we savor the moment and take things one day at a time. Yes, we are fond of talking about our future plans, but it is mostly vague and full of positivity. But the details, as to what exactly will I do the next year or what course I should take in college, were somewhat left to *chance*. Believe it or not, I only learned I am going to become a doctor just a few months before I actually applied to medical school, thus the non-medically inclined bachelor of art degree in psychology as my pre-med, rather than the more medically-related ones like nursing, medical technology or biology.

And as it turned out, having gone through various twists and turns actually did give me some advantage. For instance, I was able to develop my drawing/painting skills outside of school, which later helped me in studying anatomy. In psychology, I developed my skills in human interactions while at the same time had in-depth training in research work, and these skills also contributed to how I survived the medical school pressure despite the academic challenges. Living independently since high school, I was able to experiment with recipes and eventually developed my own. As a result, I became a medical doctor and a surgeon, who commissions artworks, with a side hobby involving food, plant and arts/craft business, who does research, writes books on health and wellness and is still constantly evolving and learning to do something else. As you can see, you are welcome to allow yourself to have more than just one career path. It may take trial and error and some risk assessment, but in the end, you are more likely to discover or develop certain aspects of yourself that can advance your skills way more than you do now.

Others call it passion and most often, they separate it from their job. And I believe that you can have both, or even more. Thus, I am not telling you to quit your job and just blindly do what you are most passionate about. Instead, you can take a step back to see your life clearly and focus on what is most essential without jeopardizing your basic needs. If, after some thinking, you still find it difficult to choose what career path you should maximize your time on, you can start by analyzing which field you have the most experience. You can have more than one. After ranking, try to think which of them you felt the most sense of fulfillment. And lastly, which of these can also support your basic financial needs, the one that also puts food on the table. If you have all that in a certain line of work, then you might consider that road. However, if not all of these things are met, the expertise, fulfillment and money, you can choose whatever that can offer you the most. For example, the one that you have the most experience can give you money, but not fulfillment. It is then at this point where you can consider having an additional path where you can find the fulfillment that your current job might not give – something you can do during your spare time for something more fulfilling.

You have the option of continuing your day job while at the same time having a sideline that you can do after your regular working hours. Remember the Pareto Principle and how you can maximize it to your own advantage. And if it doesn't work, find another job that has it all or start a business where you can be your own boss.

Again, there is no point now of blaming the lack of a diploma or unfinished degree or wrong course taken. You are already enough and where you are can only get better the moment you dream bigger things and work on it. You can maximize whatever you have now. Remember that education can be obtained in many places and it is not only limited to schools.

If you wish to have multiple sources of income and profession, try to remember the *multi*-potentials that you have and try to see which of these potentials can provide you with such expertise, fulfillment, and financial stability. Focus on that and sooner or later, you'll be juggling it all like a pro.

Establish a habit wherein you dedicate time for personal growth, perfecting your craft, cultivating relationships and being of service for all forms of life. That way, you are tapping not just the energy within you, but those around you as well.

With the application of a PPP Happy Formula, you will not simply have a career, but a life mission that is more meaningful. Because once you do things for the benefit of something greater than yourself, the universe conspires to help you achieve something even better than your dreams.

CHAPTER XX

Perfecting Your Craft

"One person with a belief is equal to a force of 99 who have only interests."

John Stuart Mill

Thus, believe that you've got what it takes to succeed in this life.

Constant practice doesn't always lead to perfection, but constant correct practice will. Better yet, constant practice with continuous improvement can even polish up what was already considered as perfect before.

Fulfillment from growth is the second most authentic form of happiness one can get. As a dictum, I always hold in my heart the idea of *learning as if you will live forever, and living as if it is your last.*

Perfecting your craft and mastery of skills is a bulletproof plan that leads to success. Whether you are employed, managing your own business or still in the process of discovering your own strengths, today is the best time to put in effort in everything that you do. In this world of uncertainty and liberty, Warren Buffet poses a question that we could thoughtfully ponder; try to think if all of your life's value is to be placed on a bet on a single entity, *"who would you bet on?"* When I first heard this question, especially looking at it from a financial perspective, I easily decided in betting on the world's most renowned financial investors or the blue-chip companies that have the most stable record when it comes to progress. But as I later realized, I fell victim to an unpopular trap of *"self-doubt"*. It is unpopular because I didn't think of myself as an option in the first place or the first 10 options for that matter. If you are one of those, who in an instant, immediately thought that you will bet on yourself, then you have my full admiration! You are one of those lucky few who have seen what it really meant to be putting a premium to self-worth. And with it, comes along the idea of investing in yourself by grabbing each opportunity to improve whatever skills you already have, or even acquiring a new one. But if you are like me, who did not consider ourselves worthy to bet on; I assure you that we are beautifully wrong.

It is because, no matter what you do or who you are, the universe has enough resources to provide us all with the best life that we could all dream of. And in order to get that, we must first take the first step of recognizing that we are worth it. What comes with it is your own personal capacity to make each of your dreams come true.

It may all sound cliché, but there is nothing more powerful than faith and optimism. Whether it is your personal faith from someone up above, belief in your own strengths, or the *secret*, or the universe or the trend in the economy, know that your faith can provide so much than we initially thought it could.

To help you perfect your craft, the following are five simple reminders that you can do for you to be better than ever before.

1. Do not shy away from the added work. Instead, take it as a challenge. Remember, only you can benefit from such repeated experience. The other agents who can benefit from your hard work are just secondary, but the experience that you will get from it is the most important benefit that you can take.

2. If you can do it better, then, just simply do it better. Settling for mediocrity once or twice has the potential for it to develop into a habit. If we are to develop a habit, it better be a good one. Thus, strive to always do better whenever you can.

3. Do reassessment of your finished project, be happy about it and try to see how you can improve it on its version 2.0. This way, you are not leaving with a heavy heart, but

a hopeful one for the improvements you can make on the next edition.

4. Aim for *"over-preparation"* and do not settle for just the *"cross-the-bridge-when-you-get-there"* mentality. Remember, whatever extra time you thought you've wasted is not a waste at all because it is also translated into extra knowledge that you now own. And most likely, such new knowledge can be of use to you in the near future.

5. Listen and learn from others. Remember, investing in yourself is not only limited to people who are freelancers or business owners. Even employees and unemployed individuals can maximize their time both at work and at home, cultivating their own personas. With the advent of technology and information availability, you can practically master anything on your own. It is, after all, a do-it-yourself (DIY) era. And what better way to start than improving our

mindset? With a positive mind, anything great is just right around the corner.

Other than these five, there are many other ways to improve a skill or even acquire one. Develop and accelerate your current IQ through practices like mental computation (*not relying only on calculators*) and using your non-dominant hand to do common tasks. These simple practices will lead to more neural connections in your brain that will eventually later translate to advancing cognitive capability. *If you are interested to know more, there are many free online exercises for you to improve your mental skills.*

The moment you had your eyes on a specific goal for yourself*, say for example, as a world renowned athlete*, adopt its identity and make the necessary **identity shift**. In a book entitled *"Atomic Habits" by James Clear*, the problem with us not reaching our dreams and goals is because we only focus on the ***process***, or worse, just the ***outcome***. The best way to attain a dream is to shift your ***identity*** as someone that has already attained it. Live each day like a world-class athlete and start doing the routine of what world-class athletes do from the moment you wake up until you retire to bed. And before you know it, your dream self already becomes you.

This mindset on how to reach goals is not only limited to individual dreams, but it can be applied to any aspects of one's life.

CHAPTER XXI

Managing Debts and Finances

"Whether you think you can, or you think you can't – you're right,"

Henry Ford

Not everyone is blessed to be born in well-to-do families. The middle class, which comprises the larger part of the population, experience financial hardships a little more than those occupying the upper part of the pyramid and a little less than those in the lower strata. One way or another, the majority still has debts and not everyone is financially free.

Coming from the working class with bouts of highs and lows while growing up, I myself have my own set of payables and financial obligations. And although currently, I am not yet as stable as

I see it in the future, I am grateful to say that I know exactly when I will be debt-free with a trajectory of increased cash flow in the years to come.

It took me some time to get to where I am right now. And I wouldn't be without the help of one of a kind people in my life, and of course, lots of positivity. To cut it short, I will share with you the *five best ways* I know for you to attain it even faster.

1. **Believe that you deserve the abundance** and that there is enough for everyone. Thus, there is no need to compete or be greedy. Be positive and what you desire will just keep flowing.

2. **Be grateful** for whatever you have right now. No matter how meager you think you have, know that it is still better than others might have. The fact that you are reading this means that you have the faculty to interpret language and understand that you are alive and well to make each day a better

one than yesterday. According to Ken Honda, one way towards an abundant life is through "Arigato Technique" or "Thank you Technique". This is done by saying "*arigato*" or "thank you" or "*salamat*" to any amount or form of money that **comes** or **leaves** your hand. Doing so will make the money available the way air is available. We can breathe it in anytime we need it and we can breathe it out to help another being when we spend it. It can generate a beautiful cycle of wealth for you and everyone around you.

3. Just **know the minimum number** and leave the rest to **fate**. Start by computing your total income and compute your monthly recurring payables, including debts and an allowance for savings that can also be used in case of emergency. Yes, you should treat your savings as well as your debts as a basic necessity or a bill that you have to pay. For example, if your monthly income is 20,000.00, subtract

your basic needs, an example is 15,000.00. This way, you will have 5,000 left for investment or be spent on a project that can still be a way to improve your current life substantially and not just superficially. If there is just enough to cover for your needs and debts, it is okay, what is important is you are no longer adding any more debt. If you live within your means, slowly, your debt will soon be fully paid. This way, if you stick within the budget, you will know exactly when you will be debt-free.

To help you lessen your expenses and maximize savings, you can apply this Japanese concept called "*Kakeibo*" or the practice of having a financial household ledger where you record your expenses. Doing so does not only improve the accounting aspects, but it also serves as a meditative act that make you reflect on your spending. The goal is to be satisfied with only the essentials in life and avoid unnecessary spending brought about by emotionally-driven purchase (*when you are too happy, too sad or too bored*) where one is most susceptible to persuasion from marketers, according to social science experiments. Always reflect on your emotional state before purchasing anything. It is said that spending in cash is a more mindful decision than using cards/cashless transactions, thus a better option. Also, when you have something you want to buy, but uncertain, you can first sleep on it or use the "*mountain test*", wherein things you are not willing to carry in your backpack in climbing the mountains are most likely not that essential. And when you buy stuff that will really make you happy, even if it is not a necessity, make sure that the amount spent on it will not be felt or just "**kurot**" (*which means small pinch*) from your overall budget and not "**dakot**" (*which means a handful*). This way, you will be most efficient in maximizing your finances.

If by any chance you already crossed the bridge of having an income that is less than your needed payables, then it is high time that you consider getting another source of cash flow. You may have underestimated yourself, but you have what it takes to make it happen.

4. **Use your *multi*-potentials to increase cash flow** while having fun at the same time. In the book *"Rich Dad, Poor Dad"*, it is said that what will make you rich is not what you do during your working hours, but it is what you do after that will define you a monetary path.

   There are twenty-four hours a day. If you spend 10 hours in your work and travel, 8 hours for sleeping, 2 hours for personal effects, you will have 4 hours left that you can wisely choose what to do with. These 4 hours can be translated into so many income-generating activities that are legal, doable and even fun for you and even your loved ones. Before, I used to spend a lot of time on Netflix, internet, TV or Movie. Now, I spend it writing, cooking goodies I sell online, do a commissioned painting or making promotional materials that can help in the business that I engage in. I choose these businesses because these are the ones that give me the most sense of fulfillment equal to or more than the amount of energy I put into it. Whenever I get tired or bored in one task, I just shift to another that is still income-generating yet more fun or enough to cut the monotony of the previous one.

Write a checklist of what you have in your possession right now and see what you can dispose or be utilized into an income-generating activity. Most likely, if you have it, it is something related to your interests, and yes, *potentials*.

Now, take your time to think of your own potentials. It may be different for you, but trust that you have it too. There are **three ways** to know what kind of potential you can harness that can be converted into an income-generating opportunity as discussed in the previous chapters. To recap, the ***first one*** is by knowing what you love and enjoy doing the most. Chances are, you've been doing it for so long that you have become an expert on it. Make it as your own *Hobbusiness* (Hobby & Business). Don't believe me? It could really be anything. I have been on that road before, but just because you know things easily doesn't actually mean that others know how to do it well too. They may learn how if they want to, but people are technically busy and there are really those who are willing to pay for the services that they don't want to do themselves. If you still doubt it, did you know that one person has been paid and is now world-renowned just because she developed a simple system for folding clothes? Yes, she is Marie Kondo and if you don't know her, you better *Google* her and be inspired by how a straightforward skill can be extraordinary when put in the right perspective. There are billions of people here on earth, and even if you only get 0.01% of it as an audience, it is already big enough for you to make a difference.

I know that it may sound counterintuitive in reference to Chapter V, but when it comes to boosting your confidence to do what it takes to improve your life, believe that *"when you are good at something, you shouldn't do it for free"* – conditions apply, of course, like not being greedy with your fee, and doing it with the intention of being of help to others while at the same time earns you a living.

The **second part** in uncovering your other potentials is by observing what other people usually ask of you. Whether it is taking their picture, accompanying them for shopping, proofreading a text, your shoulders to cry on, as an emcee for their parties or just a frequent invitee over coffee, these are all telltale signs that people know what kind of things you are good at! It may be an eye for aesthetics, a good fashion sense, great listening skill, a bubbly personality that can liven up a crowd or just a good company, these can all be translated to valuable time that has monetary equivalent when channeled the right way. It may not be as prominent in third world countries, but *dog walking* has been already a side job that earns in many places. If you are a dog lover, you can even be a dog sitter or a baby sitter for couples who want to have a night off. The point is, you have something that people don't, and there are people who are willing to pay for it. Be creative and let your imagination run wild as you discover more about yourself and putting a premium on what you can do. Be kind to others and to yourself, thus, know your worth and get the value you rightfully deserve.

Third, after all these, you are still unsure if you have the talent or skill that deserves to get paid, do not fret. With the current trends in our modern world, you can certainly have a business even without a starting capital or just a small one. Online selling and reselling only need persistence and consistency. By choosing quality products you also believe in, you can genuinely help others get the same benefits you get by providing them with truthful information. By maintaining a good relationship with your supplier and customers, a repeat business transaction is almost always certain. Others include brokerage with many products that are of help to the community, like a financial investment or a franchise or just simply provide services that others do not want to do themselves. Yes, any craft can be learned. If you must, you can even *write a book* about it. Just put your heart into whatever it is you choose to do while maintaining a positive outlook and you'll surely see that your income will just keep on flowing. Know and accept that you deserve it and it will be yours.

5. Lastly, ***live positively today while taking care of your future***. Yes, the key to a solid financial foundation does not only include managing debts and increasing cash flow, but, it is also as important that you put emphasis on ensuring your future and that is by getting insurance, both life and medical, as well as a retirement plan. It is said that one of the dilemmas now is the question of whether you die suddenly or

you live too long. And these uncertainties, although dismal, are better addressed with a financial product that provides medical care if needed, life insurance for your family, that also becomes an investment and retirement plan. Should you follow the self-care that was discussed in the earlier chapters of this book, you are more likely to enjoy that retirement fund you so deserve.

Once you have covered it all, you can thoroughly sleep at night knowing you are secure and the future only brings brighter days.

A bonus exercise to clear the energy that's blocking your abundance:

(If you have someone you trust, you can do this with, have them read the following steps for you. If not, just read it first and internalize it one by one)

Close your eyes

Think of what it is that is blocking you. Is it something related to love, money, respect or opportunity? Is it a feeling of being not enough for you to have it? Do you feel that there always seem to be blocking you to have all the things that you wanted to do?

Next, focus on that energy of inadequacy and blockade. Try to recall when you had first felt that, how young were you, who is it that made you felt that first? Or what is the source of this feeling of inadequacy or uncertainty or confusion or the feeling of not being enough? When did you first feel it? Take your time. Do not hurry. Recall even in your younger years. It is a memory usually buried deep down, even before you were 7 years old.

Once you recognize it, the source and root of this wrong negative notion of yourself, try to feel it in your body. Over the years, it became like a parasite that lived within you. It is something very heavy that you already missed noticing. Where that energy has been stored, it feels heavy - sometimes it has spread, but do try to locate its core, its source. Is it in your head, in your gut, in your heart or your back? Try to locate it in your body, where it has resided all these times.

Once located, try to imagine a light or clear energy like the sun rays coming from above and slowly clearing that block. Keep imagining that light keeps on coming and coming from the tip of your head toward that area of negative, dark energy. Slowly, imagine it gradually disappearing. Continue to allow light to come in until all the heaviness and darkness disappears.

Slowly breathe deeply and note how light you feel. The darkness you have been carrying is no longer there. It is now painless; you are now free to accept all the kind of abundance you deserve.

Lastly, thank the universe and be grateful for it and welcome all the abundance this time, knowing that you deserve it and you are enough to receive it. You are entitled to it because you deserve it.

Now, open your eyes and as you visualize the incident from the past, it is now nothing but a neutral incident. It happened, but this time, its effect is no longer there.

I hope this exercise helps you or anyone you know. You must recognize that over time, because of others' mostly unintentional acts, we shape our self-perception in a negative way. This is the time to correct that, because you are enough. You have all the right to be here. You have all the right to receive all the abundance that there is.

SECTION 7

Zen-mode, Combat-ready

"We are not human beings having a spiritual experience; we are spiritual beings having a human experience."

Pierre Teilhard de Chardi

CHAPTER XXII

Expect the Best, Prepare for the Worst and then, Chill

"Everything around us is made up of energy. To attract positive things in your life, start by giving off positive energy".

Celestine Chua

These three simple steps can be your template in dealing with future undertakings.

1. Expect the Best

As mentioned in the previous chapters, embracing optimism at the beginning of everything makes the outcome already better. This is the key to start a fulfilling life. Nothing could go wrong if you follow this line of thinking and practice it like a religion. No superstition, but pure positivity and pair it with realistic preparedness will allow you to become a walking success.

Affirmative attitudes like *love and joy* rank among the top levels of consciousness. And when one is reaching higher consciousness, the greater is your capacity to influence your surroundings. It is where your thoughts are becoming a reality. Some call it faith, while in medicine, it is called "*the placebo effect*" where, in clinical trials, approximately 15-72% of subjects that were given a placebo or empty/sugar pill who believed they were getting the real drug, actually felt the "cure" that the real drug promises, or the pain relief of the supposed painkillers. Only this time, it is no more than just their belief in it. For some, this is the work of "*the secret*" or the "Law of Attraction" that is present in the universe. And even in the cold world of science, this capacity to influence using our mind on how things would turn out is actually supported by *quantum physics*.

No matter where you look at it, a positive and powerful thought is a vital component in any endeavor that we take. Thus, visualize and embrace the best possible outcome in anything. Be as detailed as you can be. Accept that there are enough resources for everyone, and you can just focus on what your heart desires the most.

2. *Prepare for the Worst*

After which, go back to what you have on your plate and deal with it. Scrutinize every step and every aspect and address any possible loopholes that you can think of. This phase is where you summon all your fighting spirit as well as your talents and skills to ensure that you come out victorious.

In the spectrum of positivity, this is where you use *reason*, another attribute that promotes the cultivation of consciousness. Thus, even if it initially appears to be a negative trait, the use of *reason* and *objectivity* are actually valuable tools to still strengthen your capacity to manifest the best outcome that you could think of. By being reasonable, you become grounded enough that you can deal with what you have in front of you in real-time and have the control that you need to address the aspects that need adjustments.

3. Lastly, chill.

After doing all that you can within your power, both mental and physical preparation, this is now the best time to relax and allow your thoughts to become a reality. It doesn't mean that you no longer act when things aren't going the way it is supposed to.

You still stick with maximizing what you can do by taking an internal locus of control. But for all other things that are beyond your capacity, this is where you let it go. Accompany that *process of letting go* with a whisper and *strong faith* that it will all be okay. Yes, for many, it is called *prayers*, and the faith that goes with it is the very reason why it is very effective. I am not just talking about its religious component, but the unfathomable capacity of a person's consciousness is real and magical if you'd like it to be. And by entrusting this process, you relax and are at peace. And the characteristic of being at *peace* is actually the highest state before the stage of enlightenment, where you are at your most potent, yet calm state to influence any outcome that you would like to have.

Of course, I trust that whatever your desired results are, it is all in the context of the cardinal virtues of wisdom, justice, courage, and temperance. This way, you will be blessed by being a blessing to others. Do this and you will see things changing for the better each day.

CHAPTER XXIII

Acceptance, Never-ending Hope& Zen

"Don't put off living to next week, next month, next year or next decade. The only time you're ever living is right at this moment"

Celestine Chua

Getting In-touch with your Spirituality

Spirituality, for others, may sound overwhelming. But when a person seeks a sense of fulfillment that is beyond the material, interpersonal and societal constraints, then he must get in touch with his own spirituality.

In simpler terms, this is where you listen to the inner voice within you. Some consider it as a higher power governing them, giving them light and showing them the way whenever they seem to be in the dark. Some think of it as an ultimate consciousness where clarity suddenly seems to be seen in almost any aspect of one's life. The ultimate end of spirituality is **enlightenment**. And it is where one experiences a sense of elation combined with selflessness, power without the need for control, a tranquil form of security and influence without effort, all in alignment with what is good in the world.

It is said that when one reaches enlightenment, it is when he/she has full acceptance of what he is and what he is not. Yet, able to maximize his/her own potential to be the positive source of energy that makes the lives of those they touched a lot better than when they first saw it.

In psychology, this is similar to *self-actualization* by *Abraham Maslow*, the highest order of one's aim in realizing his/her maximum potential.

So, how does one transcend to enlightenment or become *a self–actualized individual*? Before I answer this, *I have to make a disclaimer that I am not (yet) one*. In truth, I am quite far from it, but I want to believe that I am on my way. Thus, what I will share with you is what I know in theory.

Across all disciplines, the attainment of spiritual development has something to do with knowing yourself first. There are many phases and *to-do* depending on the source. But my personal favorite would be these four major steps:

1. *Remove yourself from societal standards*

Unfortunately, we have to realize that much of what we want or how we define ourselves is based on the material world. If you ask yourself who you are, most people would answer their profession or line of work, gender, age, family background, experiences or certain roles they play. This may sound like a normal answer, but if you think of it deeper, these would only refer to your role in relation to the world you are living in. Don't get me wrong, this is totally okay. However, defining yourself based on external standards is the perfect recipe for a fragile mental state because who you are should not be what others expect of you, but it should be what you are always meant to be.

To be able to escape the *"tribal mindset"* our genes eventually evolved, we have to redefine our person based on who we truly are without considering possible societal judgments. Yes, this may be hard, but it is the first step that can set you free. Define yourself by what you truly desire or how you wish for the world to be. Who you are, is the amount of love that you have for your loved ones, or the amount of care you wish to extend with nature, the oppressed and the needy, or the concern you have for the wildlife. Who you are is the strength that you wish to have to fight the injustices you see every day. Who you are is the summation of the right and wrong things you did that you want to make better.

Do not define yourself by what the culture asked you to be. Do things because it is the right thing to do, and not because it is what others expect you to do. Go against the norm if you must, so long as you do not step on another person's rights. Be brave, be courageous. Be aware of your surroundings, but never lose sight of your own self and your own individuality in the process.

2. Challenge the norm

The second phase may seem to be even harder. But once you get past it, you will be able to liberate and accelerate yourself.

This is where you no longer just accept things as they are. It is where you question almost everything. And know that you have the right to do so. For you to get past this phase, you examine things to the very core. Scrutinize and dismantle any ideology you once believed in and understand why such belief evolved to what it is now. For example, why do you think the concept of marriage was formed? Or why is it that marriage is forbidden among close degree relatives? The answer may upset some, but historically, these concepts were actually just coined by modern-day men. Marriage is ideally thought of as something that has been done under the pure intention of love and commitment. But its introduction was actually for convenience and exclusivity to make sure that the resources will be protected. More of a business venture, marriage evolved into something *"magical"* that eventually became the ultimate dream of many people on this planet now. And that kind of dream, for me, is something that evolved inorganically. However, this concept has been embedded too much in our norm that going against it already feels bad.

You see, I am not saying that you should not get married, because even if at present I am not, I am actually open to it (*for the sake of convenience in legal matters with the person that I truly want to spend the rest of my life with*). But what I want is for you to know what you are going into first before you make it as your ultimate dream. Go; get married should you want it. But make sure you marry for the right reasons and not because it is what your family/friends/others are "suggesting" you to do.

And this is just an example. There are so many things in our everyday life that we do without even questioning why we are doing it. Thus, after removing yourself from what is the norm, try to create a world where you do what you choose to do and practice tasks that you truly believe in.

And oh, before I forget, the reason why in the past, siblings/cousins/close relatives can get married but now we were so brainwashed we are already grossed out even with just the thought of it? It is simply because of the difficulty in labeling. Just imagine, if you have a child with your first cousin, then, how would your child describe his relationship with his father/uncle or mother/aunt? Did you see the conflict there? That is why, as a shortcut, it's generally been banned. And I am not saying you marry your brother because I certainly won't. But I hope this time, you will be more courageous enough to question what's needed and live in a world of your own choosing, with the standard that is intrinsically **good** and **kind** and *just* and not the world that you were forced to swallow since the day you were born. You have all the right to do so.

3. *Restructuring your own norm, renewing oneself*

In this phase, you become more aware of your own person. And as you separate yourself, your own beliefs and ideas apart from what was just imposed to you by the external world, this time, you develop your own sense of the internal world. You create a new system of concepts that are not based on other's judgments, but are based on your own. When you are in this phase, not a single thing you do, you do without reason. And in each thing that you do, the reason behind is governed by universal virtues of justice, peace, joy, moderation, love, and kindness, without any one of those contradicting the other.

Who you are and what you authentically wanted to do is what you envision yourself doing if time, money and others is not an issue.

The moment you identify yourself to its uniqueness, integrate it in your day today mentality and start living a life as if you are already at your dream life. For example, if you believe that you are an athlete who inspires the world to be healthier or a kind lawyer who fights for injustice, then, you do what an inspirational athlete or a kind lawyer do. Maybe it is waking up early in the morning for a run, or reviewing the law each night, respectively. With this practice, you are already becoming who you wish and destined to be. Once this phase is established, you can proceed with the last phase.

4. Becoming your best for the greater good

After questioning all that you were taught in the past and conceptually being reborn with the new you on phase three, it is now time for you to get back to the external world. However, this time, you go back with a different lens and different yardstick. It is from this time that you improve on yourself and apply this learning to truly impact others. It may sound ambitious, but you actually have the power to make this world a better place. You need not wait for an opportunity to do it, but, let your every decision, no matter how meager, to have the core value of improving the status quo.

The secret in becoming amazing is not about what you do, but on how much heart you put into it. Know that you are a vital persona who has the capacity to influence every little living thing that you've crossed path with. It is said that once you have reached enlightenment, you have the power to move 70 million souls. Accept that we are all connected and you, doing what you do, the best way that you can do it, are helping improve this life and the lives of many in the future.

Go and become extraordinary. Be the best version of yourself. Keep yourself inspired and take action. Know that whatever you do, only you can do it the way you do. And trust that no one else is in a better place to do it than you.

Finishing those four steps can open doors in your consciousness and current understanding of the world around and inside you more than you could ever imagine. One way to cruise your way through it is through *meditation*.

I used to not believe in meditation, but I guess it is one of those things I just refused to accept because not believing is more convenient. Now, meditation is something I always look forward to doing. Once you get used to it, your mind will naturally crave for it. You will crave for the peace and quiet, or what is called "bliss" that you get with meditation. If you wish to practice it, just try to have a 10-minute ritual every morning after you wake up. The following are the steps in meditation that you may read or skip for now

{*Be in a comfortable position like sitting or lying flat, but not too comfortable that you go back to sleep. You may choose to be in quiet place or have an instrumental audio or binaural tone (available for free on YouTube or Google) played in the background during this time. In the first months, just focus on your breathing. Initially, your mind will wander off. It is okay. You do not need to abort the meditation, but just go back to focusing and slowing your breathing when you can until the 10 minutes is over. Later on, you can practice more meditative variations like focusing on your consciousness, compassion, gratitude, and joy. You may follow the visualization steps later in this chapter as a guide for a meditation that leads to manifestation.}*

Other than meditation, the simplest way is to just have **alone time**. Embrace any occasion where you can practice independently even in as simple as eating alone in a public area. Such experiences help you develop more.

Travel either in a new place or a new angle of an old place. What is important here is having a new experience to stimulate the mind. For some, traveling becomes like a natural urge and you will easily know when you needed one. Thus, always be open to it. And maximize each opportunity where you can do so because it is one thing where most has the least regrets. In addition, solo-traveling has been advocated by many. This is like hitting many birds with one stone by developing your resiliency, patience, creativity, and personality from doing things all by yourself.

Never stop learning and enriching yourself by spending quality time with people and activities that **enhance your soul**. Whether it is talking to your loved-ones and friends, or reading a good book by a favorite author, or watching a motivational video, you make sure that you make the most out of your time. Always allot an alone time to keep yourself consciously in check to correct whatever needs correction or even improve what is already good.

Visualization and Key Steps to Dream Manifestation

I am a deep believer in the power of the *universe, the law of attraction* and *resonance* and how each of us is connected to everyone and everything around us, that whatever you wish, it will be given to you.

Be the source of the abundance that you seek and that energy will resonate and will come back to you as the answer, only this time, it is in a massive form.

It can be in an instant or it can take time, but it will happen. It is said that the thing that blocks you and your desire is the negative thoughts. Thus, if you want to eliminate it, follow these steps so you are open to manifesting whatever it is that is in your heart. It is best that you do it after your meditation.

Write down your wish, no matter how absurd or impossible you think it is. The only limit is your imagination and your negative thoughts that it cannot be done. Believe that anything is possible, and feel in your heart what it is that you really wanted. Imagine the best scenario that you could ever think of in three years' time. Do not limit yourself. Imagine that you have won the largest amount of lottery and that you can have all that you could ever want for anybody that you want to share it with. Put pictures if you can. Include in this dream all kinds of goodness, including love, health, physique, and abundance.

Close your eyes and visualize that dream. Try to see it like it is in front of you; smell the surroundings, whether it has flowers or the person or new money bills, and touch it with your hands and hear the background sounds, may it be waves or birds or the laughter of loved ones. Focus on what you feel. Embrace that positive feeling. Focus on happiness and joy as if it is already happening. Savor that bliss.

Be grateful for anything and everything that you have in your life now. Name as many things you are thankful for. Even your good health or your capacity to think right and feel right. Be thankful for the people around you. Focus on the feeling of gratitude and feel it in your heart.

Remove all negativity by forgiving all that has caused you discomfort, in the past and in the future and also ask for forgiveness to anyone whom in any way, you might have wronged as well.

Surrender everything. **Trust** that a higher power, including your own personal energy, will provide what is in your heart, or even something better, at its perfect time.

Do this every day and you will see your days feeling better than ever before. Act always towards the positive and the rest will follow.

Finally, Your Heart's Desire, a Gift from the Universe

Claim it.

Know what your life vision is, what your authentic self truly wants. Have it as your north star, as a guide on how you will live your life each day. Put in harmony all aspects of your personal life (health, fitness, intellect, and emotion), extra personal life (romantic, social and familial relationships, career and finances) and spirituality. All of these you can succeed altogether and one need not be sacrificed.

Do not shy away from accepting abundance. Trust that you deserve it, especially that you will use such abundance to also help others. Always consider yourself as an instrument to become the agent of change that can make an impact to improve the life of any living thing here on earth. Do it while at the same time committing in yourself the practice of continuous improvement or *"Kaizen"* and humility, knowing that no one is above anybody else because we are all connected in this life. Once you have accepted this sense of security and positivity with your being, only then when joy, love, abundance, peace, and contentment will just keep on flowing. These and more are the things I wish for you.

About the Author & the Cover

I am Grace and I am an *ambi*vert, with a degree in Bachelor of Arts in Psychology who eventually ended up as an *ENT Specialist - Head and Neck Surgeon*.

Internally, I am a firm believer of the power of positivity, with many of the principles I later learned to be consistent with that of Buddhism, while consciously trying to practice the cardinal virtues of Stoicism which includes *wisdom, justice, courage,* and *temperance*. With these as a guide in facing life's obstacles, like *waves*, unpredictable and strong, coming from all directions at any time of the day, the impact of stress is braced with a core that is stable, intact and calm, as seen on the cover of this book.

I used to think I did not have any skill. And it was only recently that I realized I got my mother's flair and that is the capacity to see the light in the darkest hour, and having the faith that you can create your own light even when there is none around. And I believe that this skill is something that anyone can learn over time, including you. Yes, you can do too, and I hope that in one way or another, through this book, I have shared that with you.

Author's Message

Thank you for taking the time to read this book. If you find the need for further details, you can reach me through the following:

 | jgcrojomd@healthandwellness.info

 | Dr. Josephine Grace C. Rojo
| Perfect At Last Support Group
| Life Without Rice Group
| Health and Wellness for Less (Page)

 | Healthandwellnessforless
| The Graceful Stoic

 | www.healthandwellnessforless.info

Furthermore, if you feel that it has been of help to you and wishes for others to benefit the same; you can help by referring this book to them. And should you have an Amazon Account; it will be our utmost gratitude if you can get a copy and leave a review there as well.

Thank you very much! ☺

Made in the USA
Middletown, DE
28 March 2022